Small Business
Sales Management

19

Winning Secrets of Success

Michael Delaware

If, And or But
Publishing Company

Published by
'If, And or But' Publishing Company
P.O. Box 2559
Battle Creek, Michigan 49016 USA
www.ifandorbutpublishing.com

ISBN-13: 978-0615969251
ISBN-10: 0615969259

*Dedicated to small businesses
and the people who
manage them, keeping the
wheels of commerce rolling*

Table of Contents

INTRODUCTION

I wrote this book to share wisdom and information drawn from experiences over 20 years in small business and sales management. I have worked with many different people over the years in the field of sales, and been able to look into their lives and experiences and guide them. This book is a collection of tools any sales manager can use to boost the sales in their business and through their sales team.

To present material on any subject, one must at some point sit down and sort out the salient gemstones of the content one wishes to share. In examining my own timeline in sales and management, I hand selected nineteen different points that I had not covered in depth in my prior books, *the Art of Sales Management* series.

My first book on sales management was entitled: *'The Art of Sales Management: Lessons Learned on the Fly'* which covered valuable lessons I had learned over the years as a manager.

The follow up book was entitled *'The Art of Sales Management: Revelations of a Goal Maker'* in which I discuss in depth the important points I learned over the years about setting and achieving goals in business.

Finally the third book in that series was entitled: *'The Art of Sales Management: 75 Training Drills to Build Confidence, Excellence and Teamwork'* which discussed the subject of drilling and practicing skills one learns.

All three of these books have become quite popular in their own right; however as an author I felt that there were still some secrets about being a successful sales manager I had not been able to impart in the earlier books. This book was created to fulfill that purpose.

This new book touches on several vital tools a sales manager and small business manager should know. Applying the information shared here can and will boost any sales activity. It expands upon the *people business* of sales management.

The 19 secrets I will cover in this book address different aspects of managing a small business sales operation, and it offers insight into many different layers of that activity. The underlying purpose is to bring about prosperity in the entrepreneurial spirit for the reader, and inspire them to become successful as a sales manager and small business owner.

Applying the key points presented in each chapter in this book will add 19 new tools to the arsenal of a sales manager and lighten the spirit of the activity at the same time.

SECRET #1

Developing the Winning Mentality

What does it mean to have a winning mentality? So often one hears or reads of this concept as it relates to sports as being the end all on the road to success. What does it really mean? What does it take to have this winning mentality?

When one is winning in a game or in life, there is a sensation of momentum one has. When that momentum is interrupted, slowed or broken, it could be said that one loses that a sense of certainty of success. It is that certainty of success that one feels or knows one is heading towards could be said to be the underlying fabric of the winning mentality.

When it comes to sales and managing others in sales, a winning mentality is crucial to long term success. If one loses the feeling that one is winning, life can become a struggle. Thus we have the ages old basic dual concept of *winning* versus the idea that one is in a struggle or *losing*.

Winning Vs losing

Winning could best be described as: gaining or accomplishment resulting in, or relating to victory in a contest or competition.

Losing could best be described as: to be deprived of, or ceased to have, attain or retain something.

So when one is feeling the sensation of winning, one is feeling they are making progress and accomplishing something. When one is feeling they are losing, they do not have a sense of forward progress and may even feel a sense of retraction of any ground one has gained.

Winning = → →→(Goal)
Losing = ←←←(Goal)

The Art of Sales Management

The art of managing others in sales is to keep the team one is working with in a winning frame of mind, rather than a losing frame of mind. Many factors can come into play in the environment to shift this momentum in a single member or the whole group.

Sometimes an individual can have personal problems in their life that shifts their focus on the job, and this inhibits them from being to work with that winning frame of mind as they are having so many losses in other areas of their lives.

When this happens, a sales manager needs to be alert for this and willing to speak with the individual about it. Sometimes all a person who is struggling needs is another to confer with on their struggles, and perhaps even get a different perspective on it. Not everyone needs another to solve the problem for them. Sometimes all they need is another impartial person to talk to about it. This is where the sales manager can help tremendously by just listening.

Upper Management Decisions

Another factor that can shift the momentum on a group is a company management decision that affects the sales team in how they function. Impositions of penalties, or cutting of commissions for the same amount of work, are just a few examples. Sometimes a managing body can be so removed that they do not see the impracticality of a policy change or its impact. However it is these kinds of policy changes that can turn a winning environment into one that feels they are losing.

For example: A sales team is hired with a specific commission structure. They play hard, achieve their targets and make the company a lot of money, and achieve their bonuses for doing so. A sensation of winning is electric among the sales staff as they feel their success.

However, a removed management body sees that they are writing larger checks in payroll for the sales team, and decides they need to make cuts. Thus they modify the commission and bonus structure so the sales teams earns less for the same amount of sales previously.

Although the company made more money from the sales team making their targets in the original system, the management structure could not see beyond the larger payroll checks.

The result was the sales team instead of feeling a renewed motivation to achieve their new bonuses, and targets; they now felt that they had lost ground. A sensation of losing replaced the previous sensation of winning.

How could a management body have acted differently in the above example?

To begin, they should have looked at their receivables and intake, rather than exclusively at their expenditures and outflow. Whenever a company is making more money, there will be more expenses. To operate with the idea that an increase in expenditures is somehow wrong, without examining the entire picture, is to misdiagnose the analysis.

What they should have considered doing would be to strengthen the sales team. Create a larger bonus, new rewards, etc. Something that the sales staff could sell more, and feel they are gaining ground and therefore winning. To make a decision that cuts the ground and shortens the playing field is to open the door for a sensation of losing to take over. It can also have the spiritual defeating appearance of a 'bait and switch' by an uncaring management.

Winning is driven by Accomplishment

Remember, winning is driven by a sensation of accomplishment and forward progress. Losing is a driven by a sensation of diminishing progress and less accomplishment.

> *"Winning isn't everything. It's the only thing."*
> - Vince Lombardi

Perhaps no truer statement has ever been uttered. When one considers that forward motion often encompasses the feeling accomplishment, winning is everything towards success. No one wants to lose, even though losses are an inevitable part of life.

As a sales manager one's job is to keep the group focused on a common goal or objective, and achieve forward progress towards that goal. Making sure the group knows they are making progress is essential to create a winning environment.

Winning is therefore defined as: *that feeling that embodies progress towards a goal.* Whenever a group slides into a losing mentality, then one knows that somewhere along the line the group began to feel that forward progress was not occurring. They felt stopped, halted or *defeated*.

Knowing this is the case, a sales manager does not need to necessarily find out what happened so much as what the goal was, and get the group to make some progress towards it. Make sure the group knows they are making forward motion, and make it clear for all to see.

Certainly, sometimes it may be necessary to clear the air. Make it known that there *were stops*, and even name names if necessary to get the group to let go of the past. However, the important thing to remember is that the group must face the challenge to not just break free of what is sticking their attention to the past, but also get them to refocus on the forward progress towards the goal.

Only when a group is making forward progress towards a goal will they feel that sensation of winning.

Turning a Losing Mentality into Winning

Winning therefore can become a contagious commodity in hands of a knowledgeable sales manager. Therefore to turn a losing mentality around a sales manager must do the following:

A) Find out the last time they were winning, and what occurred to make them feel they were no longer winning. See if the time of change can be isolated. See if there was a *person that created the situation, or an event that happened* or *whatever else*. Acknowledge that this occurred, and it was not right. Get them to look at it and let go. This may require some heart to heart dialogue to bring about relief.

B) Re-focus them on the goal. This can be a new goal or an old forgotten one. Get them to look forward.

C) Show them forward progress is occurring. Do this often. Soon they will embrace the idea that they are making progress, and a winning spirit will again emerge.

D) If it does not, repeat A, B & C above until it does.

Winning is forward progress and a feeling of accomplishment towards a goal. It is bolstered by the overcoming of obstacles, achievement of milestones and the receipt of rewards along the way in order to keep the winning spirit continuing with a group. Any losing spirit can be turned around as long as the sales manager knows this formula.

To create a winning mentality in ones team as a sales manager, all one need to focus on is the forward progress towards an agreed upon goal and see to it that all the players on the team are making progress towards it. This may mean individual goals set for every team member based on their skill, or ability, but one must also keep them focused on the group goal and their contribution to it. In doing so, the sales manager keeps the reality of the team in place, and the winning fever will spread through the group as long as every member feels their contributions count to the overall success.

Winners Always Want the Ball

In the 2000 movie 'The Replacements' the American football team head coach played by Gene Hackman is speaking to the quarterback played by Keanu Reeves and he makes the statement *"Winners always want the ball"*. A comedy movie, but a good message considering.

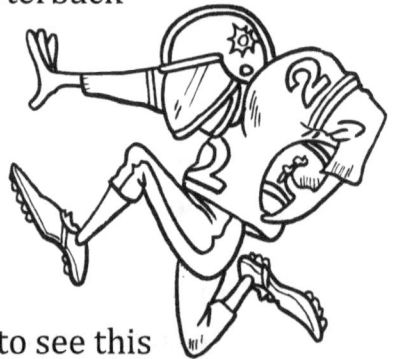

If one has ever played any kind of sports activity, it is easy to see this is true. In any sport involving a ball, whichever team is in control of it seems to be the team with the advantage. This would hold true to sports such as soccer, American football and rugby to name a few.

In sales, this concept can transcend to the subject of control. One is in control to the degree that they take charge of their own game, and move towards that goal.

The sensation of winning therefore not only accompanies the progress towards that goal, but also the feeling one is in control. Winners hold onto the ball. Winners want to be on the field in control of the ball. No one wants to be on the sidelines watching someone else doing the job for them and experience the win vicariously if they can avoid it.

A sales manager's job also includes creating the environment where every member of the team feels that they are carrying the ball. It is that one on one coaching skill of the manager that conveys to the individual that they are empowered with the control of their game, and it is up to them to win. This is how one creates a winning environment, and a winning mentality in the players one has on their team.

With a true winning mentality created among a sales force, even a setback or two cannot stop the momentum of the group marching towards their goals. This is the essence of a winning atmosphere, and it is the blaring trumpet horns of victory as the charge towards their goals.

The Difference between Pro Sports and a Sales Team

The difference between a professional sports team and a sales team is that in professional sports, no matter how good one team is versus another, at the end of the game there is always a loser.

With a sales team, there does not ever have to be a loser. The losing sensation is entirely self-created. It is a frame of mind that can be changed if the person or group can do it.

In my past books on sales management, I discuss the competition as not being just a company that is selling a similar product to yours, but instead placed it into a larger perspective. That larger perspective is the competition being defined as: *any place where the consumer will spend their dollars in the market place as opposed to buying your product.*

With this mentality, one can operate with a very wide playing field in terms of selling. In the salesperson's frame of mind, to win is to get the sale. Quite often winning simply means: *getting that sale with a specific customer.* However, if one can step above that single customer mentality for a moment, one becomes aware that there may be other customers who are equally capable of buying from them.

Thus we have a scale of awareness on sales that looks something like this:

Awareness Level One: Realization one can get a sale from a specific customer, and reach their quota if they get lucky.

Awareness Level Two: Realization that one can get the sale from multiple customers, and reach his/her quota that way with persistence.

Awareness Level Three: Realization that their quota is made by the number of people they meet, pitch and interact with daily through hard work and long hours.

Awareness Level Four: Awareness that they can make any quota, regardless of customers currently on their list or not, because they have confidence and certainty they can do it without effort and they have a constant stream of incoming referrals from their previous hard work.

Level one above could be described as where most any sales person starts out at. They are taking it one at time, and it is a much narrower frame of mind. When one climbs in viewpoint and certainty to level four, one can see it is a whole new orbit of reality.

Every salesperson can get to a point where they have that level of confidence they can get whatever they desire. It is a very special kind of awareness, and it is achieved through honest hard work with each customer, but also remaining focused on building a network of referrals.

Prior happy customers and friends who refer to a salesperson are the best source of future income. As a sales manager, there can be no greater achievement than having a team of sales people who are so well known in the community that they have a constant stream of referrals from other sources.

This is what makes the difference between a '*one team wins and the other loses*' mentality. Certainly on a level where one is narrowly focused one, losing that sale to a competitor means a loss. This 'Losing' is especially amplified when one only has that one customer on their list for the week.

To expand ones frame of mind to encompass multiple customers, and have multiple deals in motion at any given time, is to defy losing and continually win. This is how one sales person can feel they are winning, and another can feel they are losing. It is a difference in a personal frame of mind and governed by the amount of volume they are willing to handle.

It a salesperson can only handle one customer at a time; they will experience that sensation of losing more than the salesperson who can juggle many. Losing one sale to a competitor when one has many more in motion is not as devastating as losing the one and only sale one is working on.

This is the primary difference in salespeople and how it aligns with sports. Sports are the arena of contest in a single game. Sales are the arena of contest in multiple games at once. It is the single game mentality that one can slide into the sensation of losing, whereas when one has multiple games in play at any one time, one after the other, one can develop a sensation of winning.

Summary on Winning in Sales

When one is winning in sales, one is winning in life. Sales and selling is a tough profession. Some make it seem easier than others. It is really a balance of '*what volume can you juggle*', and '*how big is your field a play*' that helps one move into a winning mentality.

If you can only hold onto one customer at a time, and only see the one sale in front of you as your hope for success, you are creating a recipe for losing as a salesperson. The best mentality to develop with salespeople on one's team is the viewpoint that they can challenge themselves by having many wheels spinning with many customers at the same time.

SECRET #2

Working the Community

Sometimes a sales force slips into a frame of mind that the customer or prospect must come to them. They sit on the showroom floor and wait for that next prospect to walk in. Their very operating basis surrounds the idea that the customer will wander into their path by good fortune, and bestow a sale upon them.

This happens from time to time, and so they come to expect it. When it does not, they blame the advertising department, or the weather or the loss of the local sports team. Anyone but themselves is the cause of their present condition in sales.

A sales manager can also slide into this same line of thinking. They can clamor to the marketing department for more radio ads, more advertising and more balloons on the highway. Certainly these things work, and should be done. However a good sales manager knows that sales come from many different sources and walk-in's from advertising are only a fraction of the possible sales that are out there.

A strategy that is often not considered is to have the salespeople become involved in the community. The sales force is only so effective operating in the building where sales are made. A greater battle is getting the face of the company and the sales staff out where the people are. A great way to do this is to have your sales staff to participate in local leads groups and service clubs.

Within any community there are leads groups or service clubs. Leads groups are typically an organization of business representatives that get together and share leads on a weekly basis. Service clubs tend to have a different goal, where they come together to service a particular non-profit activity such as a children's hospital or raise money for a scholarship program for example. Both offer a setting where sales people can interact on a social level with members of the community, and in turn receive leads for new prospects either directly or indirectly from their association with the group.

Leads Groups: How they Work

Perhaps one of the most fruitful sources of generating new customers for a business entrepreneur to explore is the participation in a Leads Group. What is a 'Leads Group'? A Leads Group is an organization of individual business owners who come together at regular meetings, usually over a breakfast or lunch, and share ideas and leads for each other's businesses.

The fundamental concept is that one joins the group, usually for an entry fee, and meets with other business owners or professionals. The members help each other by sharing customers. Leads Groups can become an incredible resource to obtain customers because one is not just getting a name of a customer in need of a service, one is getting *a referral* from a member of the group. A referral is so much more valuable to the business owner than just a prospect's name. A referral is essentially Joe saying '*I suggest you speak with Bill, he is who I recommend for that service or product*'.

Customers will usually not shop once they receive a referral from someone they trust. These kinds of clients are typically the best, as the faith they have on the referrer transcends to the professional they are referring to.

What makes a Leads Groups work? Here are the key ingredients to a successful Leads Group:

➤ Every member brings at least one referral each time they meet for another member of the group.

➤ Members of the group socially interact and enjoy each other's company.

➤ In addition to sharing leads, every member has a chance to explain their business to the group at some point on the groups meeting calendar.

➤ Members share successes with others on past referrals they have received. In this way all members come to see that the system is working.

➤ Members of the group meet frequently enough to build relationships.

What are some of the rules to structure such a group? Rules for each group can vary, but here are some of the common ones to expect:

➤ The group controls its membership, and only allows one category of a business to join. This means that the group will have only one chiropractor, one Realtor, one insurance salesperson, one dog groomer, etc. This way membership in the group becomes valuable, as being in the category, one receives exclusively the leads for that profession.

➤ The group charges fees to participate. These can be above and beyond the cost of lunch or breakfast.

➤ Attendance is required. One cannot remain in such a group if one skips meetings too frequently. Commonly there are rules that limit a member from skipping a certain number of meetings per month or year before they are replaced.

➢ One is required to bring a referral for another member of the group. Sometimes points are awarded within the membership on number of referrals given. Sometimes when a group meets every week, the requirements can be that a person must bring at least one genuine lead a month.

➢ The groups tend to meet either weekly, every other week or on a monthly basis. Therefore participating in such a group requires a commitment.

When one begins participating in such a group, it can be easy to dismiss the value if one does not receive business immediately. Quite often membership shifts and changes in such groups with new people coming and going merely because they do not understand that the success in such participation cannot be measured on the short term.

It takes time for participation in a leads group to bring a return on investment. This is social interaction at its finest. Whenever one joins such a group, there is a slow curve of time that must pass before the results can be noticeable. Other members need time to get to know new people. Referrals come about from familiarity, trust and friendship. This takes time, and attendance at regular meetings for this to build. It does not happen overnight.

However, if one commits to joining such a group, it does require a change in ones way of thinking. Instead of thinking about one's own personal return, one must think in terms of helping others unconditionally. Listening throughout the week to your customers and clients for leads that might help another on your group becomes a part of life.

For example, let's assume you are a Realtor, and you hear someone at work mentioning they need a *dog groomer* for their new puppy. You should be willing and ready to take action then and refer to *the dog groomer in your group*. It may mean carrying a collection of business cards with you at the office of other members of your group, and not just waiting until the next meeting to pass along the referral.

Give out the card, and then call your fellow group member and pass along the lead to them when it happens. Then when you later attend your Leads Group, you will be able to report that you referred a lead to the dog groomer that past week, and so on. If you can commit to doing this, you will be pleasantly surprised that at some point you are receiving a call or two a month from other members of your group with leads for you.

Measuring success in such a group cannot be done on the short term. It can only be measured on the long term. One must be able to give participation in such a group at least six months before one can really being to measure the results. Additionally, one cannot just measure the number of leads received, but more importantly the gross income received. After six months did you receive only one lead, but it resulted in a $40,000 sale for your business? Let's assume participating in such a group cost you fifty dollars a month. So after six months your investment was just $300, but your return on the investment was a $40,000 sale? Imagine what it might be like after a year? What about after two years? Immediate results can sometimes happen, and you may find that in your particular industry or profession you get immediate leads. However, it is best to go into such group participation with the understanding that one cannot expect immediate return, and remain focused on the long term picture.

Some of the other benefits of participating in such a group are that you meet so many people that become lifelong friends. You can connect with the community on so many levels, and it becomes a learning experience for what is happening in the area you live and work in.

It is a great way to keep your finger on the pulse of the community, and it becomes a resource of knowledge that you can share with others to your benefit. Participating in a leads group can require a time commitment, but it can also be incredibly rewarding and develop into one of the best return on investment for your time in the long run.

As a sales manager it is important to look out into the community and encourage your sales force to get involved with a local group or activity that can place them in front of prospective customers in a social setting. Most of the time when a consumer is looking to make a major purchase in their life, they ask or consult their friends and family first. If you are in the business of selling cars, motor homes or real estate for example, if pays to have large circles of friends. The larger ones circle of friends, the greater the pool for referrals.

A salesperson should adopt the frame of mind that they cannot just rely on their own company to provide them with leads. They must also be proactive in seeking out their own customer base as well.

This is the way to sales greatness in a community. By opening ones doors to being reachable by a wide circle of friends, one is creating a greater opportunity for referrals in the future.

Service Clubs

Service clubs perhaps represent the oldest and most established organizations in Western culture. There have been many over the years that have come and gone, but there are several that remain a constant in many communities as they are connected to a national organization.

Groups such as the Rotary Club International, Kiwanis, the Optimist Club, Lions Club and many others cross genre, gender and culture in an effort to bring professional people together to meet socially and also raise money for charity.

Here are some examples:

Rotary Club International has over 34,000 clubs worldwide. Formed over 100 years ago, Rotary has over 1.2 million members worldwide. They require a referral to join, and a commitment of attendance at regular meetings throughout the year to retain membership. They strive for high ethical business standards and practices among their members, and participation in charity efforts of the group within the community. To find out more about them visit: *www.rotary.org*

Kiwanis International was founded in 1915 in Detroit, Michigan, and became an international organization with the creation of the Kiwanis Club of Hamilton, Ontario, the following year. In the early years, members focused on business networking but in 1919, the organization changed its focus to service. In the 1960s, worldwide expansion was approved and within the decade, Kiwanis International-Europe was formed, representing Kiwanians in 11 European nations. In 1987, women officially were allowed into the membership. Today Kiwanis groups can be found in most any major city in the U.S., and throughout cities in many European countries. To find out more about them visit: *www.kiwanis.org*

Optimist International is an association of more than 2,900 Optimist Clubs around the world dedicated to "Bringing Out the Best in Kids." Adult volunteers join Optimist Clubs to conduct positive service projects in their communities aimed at providing a helping hand to youth. With their upbeat attitude, Optimist Club members help with the empowerment of young people within the community. Each Optimist Club determines the needs of the young people in its community and conducts programs to meet those needs. Every year, Optimists conduct 65,000 service projects and serve well over six million young people annually. To find out more about them visit: *www.optimist.org*

The Lions Club is another global service network with over 1.35 million members in over 205 countries worldwide. Perhaps one of the largest and oldest organizations around the globe, their focus is on community betterment projects. Each club will adopt various charity or community projects to support and raise money for throughout the year and the targets can vary regionally, however the focus remains on giving to and supporting the local community. To find out more information on the Lions Club visit: *www.lionsclubs.org*

Sertoma Inc., formerly known as Sertoma International, is an organization of service clubs founded on April 11, 1912. The name is an acronym for '*Service to Mankind*'. Sertoma has clubs all over the United States and in Canada. Sertoma's primary focus is on assisting the more than 50 million people with hearing health issues and educating the public on the issues surrounding hearing health. In order to achieve these goals Sertoma has undertaken a multi-faceted approach by launching programs that address both the treatment and prevention aspects of hearing health. For more information on them visit: *www.sertoma.org*

Junior Chamber International (JCI) is one of the biggest worldwide non-political and non-sectarian youth service organizations. It is an organization of citizens between the ages of 18 to 40 with the aim and purpose of creating positive change in the world. The organization believes that these changes must result from one taking "collective action to improve themselves and the world around them." Their creed does contain a religious element; however, JCI neither promotes nor engages in any religious activities. For more information about JCI visit: *www.jci.cc/*

Soroptimist International founded in 1921 is a world-wide volunteer service organization for business and professional women who work to improve the lives of women and girls, in local communities and throughout the world. The word 'Soroptimist' was taken from the Latin words *soror* "sister" and *optimus* "best", and can be taken to mean "*best for women*". They hold the status as a non-governmental organization at the United Nations the organization claims to seek equality, peace, and international goodwill for women. The organization comprises approximately 95,000 members in more than 125 countries and territories worldwide who contribute time and financial support to community-based and international projects. Soroptimist members belong to local clubs, which determine the focus of service to their communities. To learn more about Soroptimist International visit: *www.soroptimist.org*

Apex Clubs of Australia is a network of 330 separate clubs across Australia that also focuses on community service and encouraging young people to volunteer in the community as well as develop personally. They quite often run speaking competitions and other type of events to develop life skills for young people with an emphasis on citizenship. This club was founded by former Rotary members who found some of the rules of Rotary to be too exclusionary. Up until the 1990's Apex clubs had only male memberships, but changed to allow both genders in all clubs. To learn more about Apex Clubs of Australia visit: *www.apex.org.au*

As a sales manager, one should encourage members of their team to seek out and join a service club. They must go into membership knowing it is not like a leads group. However, members of service clubs do share business with other members in the group from time to time. Being involved with an active service club can help raise awareness for one's position and business in the community, and provide connections for sales prospects.

The members of the community that take an active part in a service club generally see the benefits for their companies, organization or activity in some way and therefore are willing to help others. It can also be a great marketing resource for connections into coming events in the community that can perhaps offer great opportunities for your company.

Just like with Lead Groups, referrals from one's involvement in a Service Club can take some time and lead generation from such a group is more passive. Leads Groups tend to be more proactive with business networking, whereas Service Clubs place the purpose of the group activity before the secondary benefit of business networking. Regardless of the approach one takes, leads for a salesperson's business do flow on the lines of connections one can make by being involved in such a group.

Summary on Leads Groups & Service Clubs

It is suggested that if one has the time, they should consider being involved in both a Leads Group and a local Service Club that they enjoy. A good strategy is to select groups that will help make connections with different members of the community. This can be an important and vital strategy for any salesperson to create new business and build relationships within the community. Business tends to flow smoother among familiar parties, and being an active member in a Service Club can help any salesperson make those important connections to make this happen.

SECRET #3

Outreach with Social Media

Today with the expansion of the internet to far corners of the globe, social media has become a vibrant means of interacting with people in a wider sphere. Websites such as *Facebook*, *Twitter*, *Linkedin* and *Pinterest* among many, many other platforms for social media are a great way to reach new people.

However, as social media has grown to be more commonplace, one learns that one cannot rely exclusively on it to be a source of all ones leads. Social media has its place for salespeople, and it certainly pays to have a presence online with social media as there are some clients that use this means of communication exclusively.

It is perhaps best to regard social media as the new backyard fence where people from all corners of the planet can stay in contact, and share stories about the events in their lives. It is a way to share things that was previously done with letters through mail carriers. The nature of social media is that it is instant, and people can share information with no regard for the time zone another is in, whether or not the people it is intended for are logged in, or any other concern. Messages can be private or public, and it is the age of personal information sharing and reaching out.

With this in mind, it pays to become familiar with some of the key social media platforms and how a salesperson on your team can use them for their own personal marketing.

Facebook

Facebook.com is the largest social media and perhaps the best resource for demographic marketing ever created so far. It is more than just a place to interact with people, for the small business marketer it can be a goldmine of finding new clients if one really commits oneself to using it.

Let's examine the different aspects of Facebook:

The Personal Facebook Page

The personal page is where everyone starts on Facebook. The best practices are to make sure you have an informative profile filled out, a banner that defines you and use this to connect with friends. Examine what others in your business are doing and explore the best practices being used.

With the content you post, the best recommendation is to be positive. Express how you love your job, love the community and share friendly information. Avoid political debates, arguments or negative issues. Stay away from taking positions on controversial subject matters, and instead keep your personal page light and friendly and when possible, informative.

Make sure if you choose to support a campaign of any kind that you select subject matters that are universally appealing to everyone and are considered 'unassailable' for someone to object to. Here are some examples of unassailable topics:

- Protecting children
- Caring for pets and helping animal shelters
- Caring for the elderly
- Gardening
- Cleaning up the environment such as litter pick-up campaigns, etc.
- Home improvements
- Donating to or helping a charity

Additionally on your personal page, take time to explore Facebook in your community and like local businesses and even in some cases people in the same profession as you that you might interact with, as in the case of Realtors, educators, etc.

Always take time to post as yourself on your personal page, rather than have someone else do it for you. Make the messages personal and real. Humor also works great, but make sure it is clean and light hearted in its content. You can share information from anywhere on the internet, including articles and pictures, but make sure you post a note along with it to make it personal.

Realize that whatever you share on Facebook or in any social media vehicle can usually be seen by anyone, so consider it a broadcast and make sure that broadcast reflects professionally on you and your business at all times. Additionally Facebook has rules established about promoting your business on your personal page. It is suggested you read the rules so you understand them, so that you do not violate them. If you are found to be in violation of the rules you can have your personal page cancelled.

Facebook Groups

There are many Facebook Groups out there. Find ones that interest you and join. Post messages or articles about your company, but make sure you read any group rules first. Some groups are more open to certain types of postings than others.

Follow the rules or you will get booted and this can also become a negative on your business too. People who frequent or run groups sometimes will toss out violators of the rules, and sometimes make an example of them by posting negative content about them. So be careful and ask permission from the group manager if you are uncertain if what you want to post is appropriate.

Facebook Groups can be created by anyone. If you do not find a group that suites your interests, then create your own. As a group administrator you can set the rules, promote and monitor the group. You can also add membership from your friend base, and they can opt out if they are not interested.

Groups allow you also to hold events and post information about your business if you are the administrator. You can also invite people to join as well by posting the link to your group on other similar like minded group pages, etc.

Facebook Business Pages

Facebook has established a vehicle for businesses to openly promote their businesses. It is called the Facebook Business page. Instead of building a membership as is done with a group, a business page is driven by 'Likes'. As a small business marketer you should set yourself up a Facebook Business page and ask all your friends to 'Like' it. This is where it is important to build up a group of friends on your personal page. Once your business page has 30 'Likes' you can request a customized URL that reads as an example: '*www.Facebook.com/'Yourcompanyname*'. This specialized title can be useful and important to use along with your website in advertising anywhere online or in print.

In setting up your business page, be sure to include a banner, a detailed profile of your business information, etc. If you have a retail or storefront of any kind, you might consider using a photo of this along with a photo of your company sign for starters. If you are your business, then a personal photo of you would be important to include as well.

Facebook business pages allow you also to create and post events. You can also use applications to schedule future postings of events and articles up to a year in advance, so it does not require that you be online every day. It becomes a great way to share constant information about your business.

Facebook business pages also offer a feature called '*Facebook insights*' where you can see statistics on the success of your page. It will tell you right now how many people have seen your page that day, and in the future are expected to give you even more information including 'who' saw your page. This is a great feature to be able to monitor the progress and exposure of your business page.

Facebook mobile apps

Facebook can be accessed through most any mobile smart phone today. You can use apps to post to your personal page and also use apps to post to you business page.

There are also apps and websites that allow you to post to multiple forms of social media which we discuss later in another chapter which allow you to schedule your social media out as far as one year in advance.

The important things to remember about posting from a mobile app to any form of social media is you be very careful about the auto-correct feature on most smart phones.

There are settings that allow you to disable this if you choose on most phones. However, simply making sure you read through your post one last time before posting it is the best advice for a standard of practice. Large fingers on small key pads combined with the auto-correct feature can result in some unwanted and embarrassing messages being posted if you are not careful.

Facebook Advertising

Facebook also has one of the greatest and exciting forms of advertising ever created which can be utilized by the small business marketer. They allow businesses to post advertisements that target specific searching and profiles of people so that you can more precisely reach your clientele. If you are interested in posting an ad on Facebook, it is recommended that you click on the links for to post an ad and read the different terms available.

A small business can use this method of advertising to reach new clients geographically and within precise demographics to create powerful advertising campaigns for very little money. Combined with the *Facebook Insights* feature, a small business marketer can easily monitor results.

Twitter

Twitter.com is a tool that can best be described as a *billboard* to the small business marketer. It has also been described as 'micro-blogging' with its limitations of 140 characters or less. It has become the resource of information that anyone can find connecting all forms of social media together. News media use this as a means of getting feedback from various people in society on topics of interest and current events.

Creating a twitter account is very simple and only requires an email to set it up. Once an account is created it becomes necessary to learn how to compose messages and what to 'Tweet' as these messages are called.

What should you 'Tweet'?

For a small business one can tweet messages about all kinds of information on what is happening in and around your business. The important thing to understand is that whatever you tweet other people can see and find it, so make sure it is salient and important information that you would want people to know.

Twitter is a vehicle to post not only messages, but also links for articles, videos, photos, etc. So if there is a current news story on your business, you can post the link, for an example. Here is a list of some types of items a small business marketer could consider for Tweets:

> ➤ Photos about the business and activities
> ➤ News articles
> ➤ Videos
> ➤ Coupons
> ➤ Events
> ➤ Product information
> ➤ Specials
> ➤ Any changes in the industry
> ➤ Updates of any kind
> ➤ Helpful tips

The #Hashtag

The 'Hashtag' is the number symbol '#' on your phone or computer keypad. It has become part of the Twitter language referred to as the *Hashtag*. Placing the # symbol before a subject word or phrase such as **#Christmas, #Music** or **#Lovemydog** will enable people to search that hashtag word or phrase and find out what other people are tweeting about that subject.

As a twitter user you can create a *hashtag* about any subject and include it in your tweet. It may take some time for others to pick up on it and use it, but you can encourage your customers to tweet their satisfaction by using your hashtag for your business such as **#Joesgarage** or **#Lindasflowershop** as an example.

Hashtags allow you to trace certain subject matters and even research with twitter. Using this as a tool can give you a feel for what your customers are talking about or what is popular in general in the Twitter universe.

If you want to find out more about popular and common *Hashtags*, go to **Hashtagkey.com**.

Shortlinks

Links for certain articles and even videos can be quite long. Twitter limits you to 140 characters. This can sometimes prohibit you from talking about a subject and adding a link if the link is too long. To solve this, the *'short link'* was created. You can take any link on the internet and create a short link with it by using a link shortening tool. Simply search Google or Yahoo for 'URL Shortener' or 'Mini URL' and you will find one to use. It is a quick and easy tool to shorten a link and post it in a tweet.

Timing & Scheduling Your Tweets

To create a small business campaign for your company, you can prepare tweets and schedule them to tweet automatically in advance. The easy way to do this is to use websites and apps such as **HootSuite.com** or **Tweetdeck.com**. These websites allow you to write your tweets out and schedule them in advance. You can tweet hourly, daily, weekly or monthly depending on your strategy. You can schedule tweets for up to a year in advance. There is no limit to the number of tweets your can schedule.

It should be noted that **Tweetdeck.com** limits you to tweeting your specific message only one time. So if you have a message you would like to repeat, then you either need to vary the wording slightly or use **Hootsuite.com**. Both Hootsuite.com and Tweetdeck.com allow you to use the application for free, but offer more product services if you pay for the upgrade.

There are other services that you should explore that allow you to schedule your tweets. Some are more sophisticated than others. Some charge for their services after a free trial, and others are free but offer more when you upgrade.

Most all of these will allow you to send scheduled postings for **Twitter** and **Facebook** and some also for **Linkedin** and other social media. Be sure to read through the product descriptions, details and pricing and try them out before you commit. Find the one that is right for you.

Here is a list of some other scheduling websites for social media:

- *Twuffer.com*
- *Bufferapp.com*
- *SproutSocial.com*
- *StreamSend.com*
- *LaterBro.com*
- *Twaitter.com*
- *FutureTweets.com*

There are several more products out there and new ones being created all the time. Explore and use the one you are most comfortable with. Choose one that seems to work the best for your marketing campaign. The most important aspect you are looking for is one that allows you to schedule your tweets weeks and months in advance and sends them reliably every time without error.

Twitter Mobile

You can use Twitter on your smart phone and post tweets through right from your phone. If you use this app, once again be sure to double check your tweets before you click send.

Auto correct features on phones can change the entire meaning of your message and create an unprofessional appearance with your tweets. Also it is easy to make mistakes with large fingers on tiny key pads too.

Many of the Tweet scheduling software also offer mobile apps which allow you to work on future tweets right from your phone. So this can be a great time management tool to consider for downtime when you find yourself waiting for appointments, etc.

Linkedin

Linkedin.com is in fact one of the older more established social media websites, predating both *Twitter* and *Facebook*. This is a business networking service. The intended use if to create and connect with businesses through this professional networking social media service platform.

Linkedin like *Facebook* offers groups and like *Twitter* allows you to post messages, articles, etc. However you will find that the business groups and special subject groups are must more useful to you as a small business marketer. Here you will find groups that offer a wealth of professional experience and information in their discussions and postings. Consider Linkedin as a great resource for information, in addition to creating a professional profile for yourself and your company.

Linkedin also can serve as a professional network spanning many different companies for referrals to your business. Use it to post and share professional information about your company.

Make sure your profile has not only your contact information, but also your achievements, awards, websites, blogs, etc. Use it as your professional calling card for presenting yourself before a professional community. Be willing to share leads with others as well.

YouTube

YouTube.com is sometimes overlooked when considering social media entities. However, it is in a whole new dimension of social media. **YouTube** uses videos as a way of creating interchange and sharing information. Millions of videos are uploaded and shared on **YouTube** daily.

This can be a great resource for you and your company to get out information about your products and services. Videos can be created and uploaded from a smart phone or laptop computer. There are all different levels of video editing software out there to help you get started with editing your own videos.

YouTube also has tools online that allow you to edit videos. If you want to invest in some professional video editing software and cameras, you can do that as well.

In addition to that, you might consider hiring someone to create and produce them for you. However, this last method can be more expensive, but might be the best route for a truly professional presentation.

The best suggestion for finding the right method for you is to go to **YouTube** and watch videos on 'How to create videos' until you discover the method you are most interested in using for your marketing campaign.

Pinterest

Pinterest.com is one of the newer social media networks that is catching on with large popularity so it is worth mentioning to the small business marketer.

Pinterest is a social media website that allows people to share photos and images with as much ease as Twitter. It allows you to organize items of interest in picture or image format, and share the things that you love and are inspired by in short descriptions of the images.

Small business marketers are using **Pinterest** to show photos of their products and include a link. One can also share images that are quotes in a picture form, and post those with a link as well.

You can use **Pinterest** for commercial use, and they state on their website the following: "If you want to use our Products for commercial purposes you must create a business account and agree to our Business Terms of Service."

So as with any form of social media, read the terms of use and follow the required practices for business to promote within their guidelines. **Pinterest** can be a great tool to share interesting images related to your company and install a link to more information billboards and redirect to other articles as well. It can also be a simple and easy way to create interest for your products and services.

Social Media Summary

Social media is always evolving. One can say that the constant in social media is that there is *no constant.* 'Change' is the only thing one can come to expect. Social media platforms grow and evolve, and some die off and are replaced by others that are new and more exciting.

Demographics change for social media platforms as well. For example, Facebook in the beginning was largely a younger age group using it, and now the medium age group is more in their 40's and 50's according to recent news articles.

The only way to stay ahead of the changes is to be involved actively in social media, and make a commitment to having it become an active part of your small business marketing plan as a salesperson. If you do not, then it will pass you by.

Always read the terms of service and use of the various social media platforms you are using. Follow the rules or they can terminate your account and you will risk losing all of your contacts.

Try to use social media as a tool to meet new clients and stay in touch with former ones. It has grown to become such an integral part of the culture in this internet age that the small business marketer cannot ignore it. It is where people are spending their time, even at work. So if you want to reach them you need to be where the customer can be found.

As a sales manager, it is a good thing to encourage the use of social media for the purpose of generating leads for your sales staff. If they are going to be actively representing the company, it might be prudent to set up some ground rules on what someone can post regarding the company and its products.

SECRET #4

Drawing Together with Sports

As mentioned in my earlier books on sales management, sports offer a great correlation for the field of sales. It is easy to describe a sales environment to a new person by using sports as a comparison. There is the challenge, the individual performance and also the team activity.

As a sales manager, one can use the analogy of sports to draw a group of sales people together as a team. It can make the activity challenging and competitive, yet fun as well.

Using sports as an analogy offers the following perspectives for a manager to apply to the group:

> - *Sports offer an opportunity for individual performance and excellence.*
> - *Sports offer an environment where players can work together as a team to accomplish something.*
> - *Sports bring about the reality of winning and losing, and the drive to win.*
> - *Sports offer an understanding of limits on time, the challenge of distance and the demand for excellence.*
> - *Sports offer a sense of competition.*

A sales manager can use each of these points to bring together a cohesive team of sales people who develop an understanding of games.

Games

Games could best be defined as: A form of play or activity, especially a competitive one played according to rules (detailing boundaries, distance and conduct) and decided by skill, strength or luck.

On the surface, games have two basic parts: *components and rules.*

1) Components could be said to be the physical barriers and guides that one agrees to play the game on. In a board game for example, the components would the game board and its pieces. In soccer it is the field, the markings on the field, the goal, the other players and the ball.

2) Rules define the agreements to follow in the course of play. It lays out how each player and piece may be used in the course of contest or activity.

When one looks further into this, one discovers there are essentially six main component parts to a game that make the activity interesting to all involved:

- ➤ Rules
- ➤ Components
- ➤ The Goal
- ➤ The element of chance
- ➤ Competition
- ➤ A willingness to play

In looking at these five parts we can see that if there were no *rules*, there would be no sense of order to the game. If there were no *components*, there would be no barriers or field to play on. If there was no *goal*, no one would know what the objective was. If the *element of chance* were no present, it there would be no ambition to explore the outcome. If there was no *competition*, it would lack the challenge of playing against others. If the players are not *willing to play*, there is no game.

We can examine any existing sport such as football and we can see each of the five elements above. *There are rules in football*. One cannot step out of bounds, or continue play after the whistle is blown for example. *There are components.* One must have a ball and a field to play on. *There is a goal.*

One is trying to score a touchdown at the other team's end of the field. *There is the element of chance.* One really cannot predict the outcome of a game, as there are so many variables. *Then there is the competition.*

Two teams playing against each other with the determination by each to emerge the victor. Finally, both teams of players must be willing to play, or there really is no game is there?

Summary on Sports & Games

Understanding games can help a sales manager to establish a game among salespeople that they will play. Embracing the willingness to play therefore is also a part of it. Games strike at the nature of mankind and most anyone enjoys playing some type of game. No one wants to play a game they are not willing to play. The challenge for the sale manager is in finding the right game everyone will play.

SECRET #5

Capturing Leads at the Close

A valuable asset to any sales manager is a sales staff that is trained in capturing future prospects at the closing table.

One would be surprised at how many companies do not consider the importance of prospecting at the closing table. Some do not even consider the idea that it can be done.

Prospecting at the closing table is a simple routine. It is a regimen where the salesperson routinely asks for prospects from every customer they close. If done correctly, it can be a vital resource for collecting a seemingly endless supply of future prospects.

How does a system like this work? Where do you start?

Capturing Leads at the Close

This is a very simple technique. It is so simple, that as you read through this one might be inclined to think 'Ah! *Why didn't I think of that?'*

Here is how it works, step by step:

1) At the closing of whatever the product is (car, real estate, boat, home improvement product, etc.) the salesperson carries with them a small stack of 3 X 5 Index cards.

2) At the appropriate moment when all the business is attended to, you say to your client *"Oh, one more thing"* as you slide five or six of those blank 3 X 5 index cards across the table to them. *"Can you take a moment and write down a name on each card of person you think could also benefit from the same _____ you just purchased?"* (Or similar wording).

3) You are simply looking for them to write a name on each card, and hand it back to you. If they need more than the 5 or 6 you gave them, give them more.

4) Once they have done this, ask them if they have their phone numbers. Then ask them to write that under each name. (If they do not have a phone number, try to get some other point of contact like an email, mailing address, etc.)

5) Then take all the cards back, and lay them all on the table in front of them with the names facing them. Then ask them *"Of all of these names, which do you think is the best one for me to call?"*

6) They will tell you one of the names. Sometimes they will tell you two. Ask them if they are certain that this is the best one. Once they agree it is, ask the magic question: *"Would you mind calling this person for me and introducing them to me right now?"* and hand them a phone.

7) If you have taken care along the way to maintain the friendly relationship, and keep the interaction light, they will most often comply and make the call right then and there for you. If not, they may offer to call him for you by a specific time, whereas you can call the prospect after that, and it will serve as an introduction.

So examining the above seven steps to prospecting, there are some obvious questions. You might ask, why just ask him for the best one? It is simple; this one is most likely the hottest prospect in the lot. Work the hottest prospect first. What do you do with the other leads? Call them of course, or pass them off to an assistant if you have too many leads to work.

If you implement this system with all of your sales staff, they might likely find that they are getting 6-10 leads from every customer. If a team is selling a lot of transactions, they can quickly get flooded with leads, and then it becomes easy to neglect them. Therefore with this system, it requires at a minimum that they focus on the best lead in the lot they get from each prospect. When they are selling a dozen sales a week, and applying this system, the number of sales will increase.

Let us put it into the context of car sales. Let's assume a new to moderate salesperson is selling an average of 12 sales per week, and then let's look at these numbers:

- 12 sales a week X 6 leads = 72 leads.
- 1-2 hot leads out of 6 in every 12 sales = 12 to 24 hot leads

With this system in place, the sales people could potentially boost their individual sales to say 30 per week. Then the numbers would look like this:

- 30 sales a week X 6 leads = 180 leads
- 1-2 hot leads out of 6 in every 30 sales = 30 to 60 hot leads

With a quick comparison, and an understanding on what it truly takes to follow up on a lead when one is busy one can see that it is better to have the system in place where the focus on the hot leads first. Why? Because that is the lead the customer who knows the prospect has identified as most likely to make a purchase.

The other leads have value, but more of a secondary value in the pool of leads. They should be called, but only after the salesperson has called all the hot leads first. When one gets really busy, it pays to focus on just the hot leads in this system. When one slows down, then pull out the drawer of secondary leads and burn up the phone lines.

This system for prospecting at the close is a successful one which relies on good customer relations. It will not work if the salesperson has not built a relationship, and becomes too mechanical with it. It should be a comparison to that of a friendly conversation between friends.

It is a very simple approach and it generates leads that are worth pursuing. This method can be modified to your company needs and products, but the concept is the same. One simply asks for the customer at the closing table when they are at their peak of satisfaction and excitement about their purchase to provide you with some prospects. If you do not ask, you will not get the leads.

It is common for people who are buying to want to share their success with others, and may not at the time think about who they would tell or recommend for a similar purchase. What the salesperson is doing here is cutting out the time from their having this realization and getting the information now.

Summary of Capturing Leads at the Close

It is a very easy system to implement, but it does take some courage at first. Getting past that point of unwillingness or fear of asking is usually the first hurdle. Once one plows ahead and tries it, and has some success with it, it will become a regular mainstay of a system for capturing prospects at closing that every sales manager and salesperson will enjoy.

SECRET #6

Know Your Customer, and then Know Him Again and Again

Any sales manager will tell you that part of the success of running any sales force is to know the customer base. Sometimes however, one can get into a frame of mind that they have their entire customer base figured out and understood. This kind of thinking is limited, and can actually become a trap for a sales manager.

If one assumes they know the customer completely, then next logically step one takes is to stop trying to know their customer. You see how that works? One adopts an attitude of complete understanding, which is really an assumed understanding, as one has ceased to try to understand. Therefore as times change, one finds their company is more distanced from their customer, and they soon experience a decline in sales.

Why does this happen? One assumed they knew everything and stopped trying to learn. That is all that happened.

This lesson is easy to see in the collapse of major companies in recent times. Let's look at a few examples of this:

Blockbuster Video: A perfect example of a company that knew and understood their customer at one point, and built great success upon it, the failed to continue to know their customers. The company became outdated with the rise of competitors like Netflix who offered videos through the mail. Cable and phone companies started offering videos on demand. Redbox started renting videos for a dollar overnight through vending machines, and video streaming through the internet made it easy to rent videos without leaving the house. Blockbuster failed to adapt, and explore the needs of the customer as they evolved, and thus fell behind and lost their customer base with stores that soon became dated and out of touch.

Eastman Kodak: With the introduction of the Brownie camera in 1900, no company has been more dominant in any field like Kodak was to cameras for almost a hundred years. However, with the development of digital cameras and all the printers, file sharing and software that have developed in recent years, Kodak has missed out on the changes in the industry. They shifted their attention to the healthcare imaging industry, but have nevertheless fallen behind their original primary customer base which was selling cameras to consumers. Now film camera technology is almost obsolete in the amateur and professional photography field, giving way to the ease and simplicity of digital imaging.

Sears: Once a dominate business in the catalogue industry, now has lost ground to major competitors like Wal-Mart, Target and Amazon that have chewed away at their customer base for years. The Sears tower in Chicago is still called that locally, but the namesake moved out years ago and the tower is officially called the Willis Tower which is named after its largest tenant a British Insurance company. Sears lost touch with their customer base, and fell behind the changing times to competitors who continued to learn who the customer was.

Toy's R' Us – Once a major retailer thriving in the 80's and 90's, this company paraded the megastore approach in the toy and game industry with the rise of American consumption. However, with the introduction of large discount stores like Wal-Mart and online retailers like Amazon, they began to lose ground with their customer base. Today they have closed many of their megastores across the country, and are downsizing with a new strategy for turnaround launched in 2004. Time will tell how they emerge from their collapse after losing touch with their customer base.

Motorola: The first big success with this company came with car radios, and then this led to two way radios, and ultimately the development of the cell phone. Motorola had the best selling Razr phone which dominated the market not too many years ago, but they failed to continue to research what their customer needed and wanted. They fell behind with the introduction of the smart phone technology which introduced the handling of email and other data, and Motorola lost ground to companies like *Research in Motion, Apple, LG* and *Samsung*. Motorola phones were vanquished so quickly by lack of consumer demand from the mobile phone industry that their cell phone division became a perennial money loser and they eventually closed down that section of the company.

What can a small business sales manager learn from these lessons of larger companies? Essentially the most important lesson is that one can never assume they know their customers. They must seek to know their customer, and then know them again, and again. The customer is always changing and in flux, whether it is apparent or not. This is happening even faster in the age of the internet.

Times and trends are always changing in every business. What is hot today can be replaced by something better or cheaper tomorrow. Just looking at the music business where it went from reel to reel tapes and records, to 8 Tracks, Cassettes, then to CD's and now to merely digital files sold online downloaded to the iPod. This transition took place in less than 50 years, which is a mere blip in the life of any industry.

To avoid getting lost in the changing times, one must have a system in place to continually know what the needs and wants of their customers are. To do this, one must take time to find out.

How does one do this? The easiest way is to ask the customer. Set up a system of survey and data collection from customers and sales people and even prospective customers to gather as much information as possible.

Client Data Collection Plan

The best way to find out continually about your customer and their changes in buying patterns and needs is to have a data collection plan running at all times. Here is a breakdown of some of the various ways to do this:

Customer Surveys:

- ➢ Surveys through mail
- ➢ Surveys through email
- ➢ Surveys through social media
- ➢ Surveys through online coupon offers
- ➢ Direct in store surveys with customers through personal interview

> ➤ Direct survey of customers through written surveys in the store
> ➤ Customer receipt surveys

Consumer focus groups:

> ➤ Sign up customer to participate in a customer focus group and reward them with discounts, coupons, etc.

Salesperson Data collection:

> ➤ Salesperson 1 -2 question surveys of customers at closing.
> ➤ Salesperson info sheets to gather data on trends they hear about through customers
> ➤ Sales meetings with your sales staff and conduct group surveys

Suggestion boxes:

> ➤ Suggestion boxes in the store at strategic points
> ➤ Suggestion boxes online on the websites

Customer reviews:

> ➤ Customer reviews online for individual products
> ➤ Customer reviews online for the store or business

➢ Customer complaints online about your business or employees, etc.

Study and learn about new and potential changes in the industry:

➢ Sometimes new products are developed or sold by your competitors, and your business needs to carry them as well. Find out what they are by staying connected to your industry.
➢ Learn about technology or ideas from similar industries, and test application to your industry to see if you can launch a new product.
➢ Try and test other similar products on the market and borrow ideas, make changes to your products or services to compete.
➢ Read and subscribe to trade magazines.
➢ Research through social media and other online websites what new technologies people are talking about and using.

Some of the above may seem quite obvious, and others you may not have thought about. However it is the business of a small business owner and also a sales manager to know as much about what the customer thinks about your product and services including both the good and bad in order to really understand how to improve your business and stay on the cutting edge.

Businesses that seek to learn what their customers need and want and then use that information to provide it to the customers are the ones that expand and survive. The ones that do not listen and do not ask and ignore new changes in the needs and wants of their customer base soon find they no longer have a revenue stream to run a business on.

Controlling the Revenue Stream

A customer base is a revenue stream. That is about as simple as it gets. In fact the word 'currency' comes from the root word '*current*' implying that money *flows* much like a river or stream. If you can imagine one's customer base as being that river of money that one wants to control and direct into your place of business, you will have a basic understanding on the foundation of how this works.

Seeking to always know the customer, and know him or her again and again is how one controls the revenue stream. However, with knowledge it does also take some willingness to execute what one learns.

Microsoft learned a great deal about customer trends and needs, and passed up on many items such as Web TV, eBooks, smart phones and tablet PC's despite having knowledge and know-how on many of these developments before their competition. They failed to commercialize many of these discoveries, and even gave some away without capitalizing on them.

So it is not just having the knowledge and information pool, but it is also being creative with its implementation and use. Using what one learns to introduce and test new products and services is how a business grows.

Upon examination, we can see that there really are two parts to this:

Discovery → Implementation
Implementation → Discovery

Both draw from the other. One discovers new things and implements these. As one implements the new products of services, one continues to discover what the consumer wants and needs as they use the new product or service.

When the first VHS recorders came into existence, it was in the early 1980's. The first ones were built to be large and took two people to carry them and they cost around $2000. By the late 1980's they were replaced with smaller more portable models, and the prices were greatly reduced to the $300 range. By the early 90's one could purchase a unit at most any store for under $100. The VHS technology was eventually replaced with DVD, and the DVD is now giving way to BlueRay Disks, which it giving way to Web TV and other direct viewing services.

Each new product goes through a cycle of discovery, implementation, followed by more discoveries and then more implementation and so on. Compare a television of the 1950's to the flat screen TV's of today. Compare the rotary telephone to the mobile smart phone of modern times.

Summary on Knowing the Customer

Almost any product or service can and will eventually evolve; some will be faster than others. However, the business that can learn about the customers and their needs as times change will be on the cutting edge of their industry. The ones who do not will be left behind.

SECRET #7

Brilliant Special Events

Small business owners and sales managers know the magic of hosting events at a retail place of business. The trick is to be able to host a brilliant event which not only draws people to the store for sales purposes, but also has them leaving the event talking about the business to others. This second part is called 'word of mouth' and an event that can create *word of mouth* advertising after it is held is a *brilliant event.*

The way to do this is to host an event at the store or business location. If you have more than one store, it can pay off to host a private or open public event at many locations. Special events can draw traffic to the location that can result in future sales and a raised public awareness of your business in the community. They can also help to generate that infinitely valuable after effect of *word of mouth* promotion.

Categories of Events

There are two basic categories of events.

1. New business opening events
2. Established business events

Within each of these two categories there can be both *private* and *public* events which can open the door to new customers and clientele.

A private event involves inviting a specialized group of people generally through personal invitation. An open public event generally involves much more fanfare and promotion to draw anyone who will come.
Setting up a Successful Private Event

Setting up a private event requires coming up with something to draw interest. It also requires having a mailing list to send invitations to. These invitations can be sent to a list of personal friends, or a select group of people in a particular category. One can acquire a mailing list as discussed in the earlier chapter on Direct Mail. Select a group of people that are likely to respond to your personal invitation.

Drawing Interest

Drawing interest to the event requires what is coined in public relations circles as a 'gimmick'. 'Gimmicks' are usually intriguing things that will capture someone's interest and compel them to arrive. Here are some ideas of gimmicks for a private 'invitation only' event that can draw people:

- A celebrity or some other popular public figure
- A wine tasting
- A private chef cooking some unique food
- Good food or cuisine
- A magician
- Musicians & music
- A unique form of entertainment
- A special lecture on a topic of interest
- A popular cause
- A radio personality
- A contest or reward
- An awards ceremony (where the invitees are likely recipients)
- A special private unveiling of something new and never before seen
- A mystery to invite imagination

The above is just a list of ideas that have proven to work. There is no limit to the creativity once you start brainstorming on it. The essential characteristic of a good private event is that the feature or 'Gimmick' is *too irresistible to pass up.*

It is always important to have something that keeps people there as well. Food is always a good draw and can keep people around. The same goes for a wine tasting or popular personality. One can look at the list above and incorporate more than one in the same event to make it even more compelling to attend.

One should of course have staff of your business present and displays or information available about your company for all guests. Present the information in a tactful manner as part of a gift when they arrive, information brochure, etc.

It is important that such events start on time, and end on the time as well. One should also check invitations at the door to make sure at least the illusion of exclusivity is presented even if you do not want to be strong on the enforcement of it.

An example of a private event I once held in my Decorative Glass Company in Atlanta was the following:

We invited a well known and high priced interior decorator to come in and do a presentation. We set up a slide projector and screen, and invited her to do a talk on interior decorating. As an introduction to the speaker, we presented a short ten minute slide show on stained and decorative glass applications for the home, showing photos and providing them free information. We also included some small amounts of food and snacks from a local catering company, along with some coffee and tea. All attendees left with a special folder which included business cards, flyers, coupons, etc. from our company and our guest speaker. We also had a violinist playing in the reception before the event started. We started on time, and ended on time.

The events were held around 7pm each time. We held this and similar events over a period of six months with different speakers. Each event we had approximately 20 to 25 attendees. This size of group made it possible to answer questions, and interact with them socially on a more personal level. The end result was that both our speaker and our company got business from the event, and it became a regular part of our successful actions.

This event came about from a brainstorming of our sales staff and surveying our customers. They were always well attended and the word of mouth spread the more we did them. We invited people from specific neighborhoods as well as from our own customer files to generate repeat business.

There can be many variations on such an event, and it does not have to become too costly. There is always some expense and a preparation involved, but the outcome can be well worth it.

Here is an example of an event held by the Public Relations Director at Atlanta Homes & Lifestyles Magazine in the 1990's:

A contest was held in the magazine for interior designers to submit photos of their work for a contest. The magazine staff would review the entries and give out awards in different categories, as well as one large overall award for 'Designer of the year'. They then set up the event at the small business of one of their advertisers and held an awards ceremony. When interviewing the PR director afterwards he said "If you ever want to have 100% attendance, hold an awards ceremony and invite a large group of potential winners'. So this was the format for their event.

They of course had food, wine, music and a lot of fanfare. They gave out awards in numerous categories from 'Best Contemporary Design', 'Most Original Design', 'New Trend Setting Design', 'Best Traditional Design', etc. Of course there was also the overall prize of 'Designer of the Year' as well. It was a great event and a packed house.

The event was held in the showroom of a kitchen design company, and they of course benefited from the exposure to all of the Cities best interior designers that evening in their newly opened showroom.

As a result, they continued to advertise with Atlanta Homes & Lifestyles Magazine, and the magazine also signed up new clients that night too because they invited prospective advertisers to attend the exclusive ceremony and meet the Cities top designers.

Holding a Successful Open Public Event

Public events are ones where you are trying to draw people from a larger base, and are not selective about where they come from; you are just trying to generate broad exposure for your business. These can be great events for launching a new business or just giving a boost to an already established business.

Once again having a 'gimmick' that will appeal or attract the broad masses is essential. One needs to set up the event so that it will attract people from visual drive-by, radio & television, print media and other forms of display advertising. One cannot take an 'ordinary' approach and expect people to pay notice. The small business marketer needs to think like a three ring circus and try to attract on many levels.

Here are a few creative and radical ideas that have proven to be attention getting. Use as many as you can, and also explore and look for other creative methods when you find them:

Radio broadcast – Quite often radio stations in the area can be contracted to come and do a live broadcast from your store. These can vary in price, depending on the size and popularity of the radio station. This usually involves a radio personality or personalities broadcasting their entire show or a portion of it live from your business. They of course invite people to come visit them and see your business, take part in the live show, etc. This is quite a fun way to draw people. It is suggested that you do a survey of any existing customers you might have and find out what radio stations they listen to. Radio stations tend to appeal to different demographics, and their marketing and sales department should be able to provide you with information on this.

Radio 'Prize Patrol' – This is a step down from an actual broadcast. Many radio stations have a van with their logo on it that travels around and sets up at businesses in the area. They call into the station during broadcasts and let people know where they are located and ask them to come on down to win cool prizes. The advantage of a prize patrol is that they often are a lot less costly to procure, and sometimes they can stay longer. On a good weather day it is possible to draw quite a crowd.

Spotlight – If you are hosting an event in the evening, then a spot light can be an incredible way to attract attention. There are companies that rent huge spotlights that usually are on a trailer or vehicle and they bring this to the store, and shoot the beam of light from your parking lot into the sky. This works best on a clear night or a semi-clear night when there is a low cloud cover in the sky. This kind of gimmick brings the curious to investigate what is going on, so it is important to tie this in with other things that will draw them into the parking lot or compel them to stop at the store when they arrive.

Specialty Signage – Everyone loves a 'Sale'. The word 'Sale' may sound overdone, but in fact it is so ingrained in the psyche of the average shopper that it is a great draw. It works best to place these signs where they can appear temporary and also obvious. You might be surprised that a hand drawn 'Sale' sign will quite often attract more curious buyers in some smaller businesses than a pre-made one. It can give the impression of it being individual and unique in the right circumstance. Large fabric banners tied across the front of the store or flapping in the wind are also great ways to draw people. Just make sure that were ever you place them, that they are visible from both close and far away. Different sizes of signs are also important to accomplish this, and pointing in different directions.

Skywriting – There are some companies that do sky writing with small airplanes. This can be an interesting draw, however due to the limitations of the skywriter and fuel it usually limits you to a one to three word message. So if your business has a short recognizable name, you might pay someone to sky write *'Sale at ___'* in the sky. This kind of gimmick of course is limited to a clear sky day, so it can be difficult to schedule.

Airplane banner towing – This is often an easier and less expensive option than skywriting. A small airplane will tow a banner behind it with your message in circles in the sky around your store. This can be another great curiosity draw from long distances on a clear day. Choose a bright colored banner and a bold readable message to advertise your event and let it fly.

Inflatable displays - There are companies that set up large inflatable animals of all kinds to serve as big bold and crazy temporary signs for events such as this. There is also the large inflatable houses that independent vendors can set up to charge admission for kids to jump around inside.

Set up a small carnival – If you have the advantage of a large parking lot or field adjacent to your business, consider setting up small one to two day carnival. There are companies that travel around and do this for auto dealerships and other businesses, and it can become an instant event that requires little preparation on your part. The often come complete with rides, displays and other attractions.

Moving signage – There are several simple rentable signage displays that are often available through a local rental center. A particularly good one to attract drive-by attention is the portable fan that blows upwardly through wind sock shaped like a cartoon man. It flops back and forth in the intermittent wind of the fan, and has great movement to attract attention to what is going on. It helps to flank such an item with clear signage about your event to that when people look, they get the message and are compelled to stop.

Balloons – There are many types of balloons one can use to attract attention. One can simply rent a small helium tank and blow up multi-colored balloon and tie them all over. There is also the Mylar style balloon which is silver in color that reflects sunlight and moves in the wind. Then there are the large balloons one can inflate and tether and have it floating 300+ feet in the sky. Additionally one can contact local hot air balloonists and have one or more hot air balloons inflated in your parking area in front of your business. Sometimes they can be arranged to give tether rides as an additional draw. Balloons can be magical attention grabbers and have broad appeal.

Celebrity Booking – Another great public drawing gimmick is to have a celebrity on hand to sign autographs. Contact a local sports or celebrity booking company like *www.universalattractions.com* or *www.commandtalent.com* to choose the one that will be the right personality draw for your business. They can range from actors, media personalities to local professional sports players. There are many such companies, and prices for this vary depending on the popularity of the personality you hire. Two important things to consider in taking this approach: One, make sure you survey your customer demographics to choose the right personality for that demographic. Two, be certain to verify that the personality you hire has a reputation of showing up on time and not cancelling. Nothing can torpedo a public relations event more destructively than to have a celebrity you contract cancel at the last minute and ruin your event.

Freebies – Giving away free items can be a great draw, especially if it is a highly desirable or popular item. 'Free Beer and Hot Wings' or 'Enter to win a Free Tractor' etc. can be great gimmicks. I would caution any business owner on giving away free alcohol products; however, as there can be considerable liability with this should someone leave your event and have an alcohol related accident on their way home. It can also require special permits from your local municipality to do this. However there are a lot of other great food items that can be a draw such as: *chili, fried chicken, boiled peanuts, bagels, sandwiches, steak, hamburgers, hotdogs, hot apple cider, coffee, hot chocolate, lemonade, ice cream, etc.* that can just as attractive in the right circumstance and make for a fun event.

Sometimes hiring a few food vendors to set up portable booths in front of your store can also be a great draw. Prizes and contests also work well as a 'freebie' draw, and can be promoted to hold drawings throughout the day to get people to stay longer and enter to win. A popular giveaway is often an iPad or computer item, for example. Holding a sign-up entry contest can also be a great way to collect identities for future marketing, which will be discussed later in this book.

Music – Music can be another great draw. One can hire a DJ or hire a series of bands and promote them as part of the event. One can also have single musicians to play background music while people tour the store, such as a pianist, cellist, violinist or guitar player. It all depends on the theme and taste of your event, but music can be a great way to keep people around and draw them to the event as well. What is important to consider when choosing to use this option is that one choose a source a musical entertainment that will be popular to the demographics you are servicing and reaching out to in your business.

Invitations – Invitations can be sent out as a direct mail piece to a surrounding demographic area or to a select group. It is important to time this promotion to arrive at least 1-2 days before the event in their mail box. If doing multiple mailings (which is preferred for greater success) then arrange for the first piece arrive one week before the event, and the others within the following days to keep the reminder present in their minds. Be sure to include all the details of your event that can be expected: food, music, and personalities, balloon rides, etc. whatever is appropriate.

This is a list of ideas that can be used, and it is always good advice to examine other events held by businesses in your area that drew a lot of people to mimic what they are doing.

If one does not have the patience to organize such an event, there often are companies that you can hire to make all the arrangements and do all of the planning for you so you can just focus on being ready and selling your products.

Events can take a lot of preparation, but in the long run can be well worth it for the continuous exposure they can create for a business. It is recommended to have an event of some kind planned for your business as a part of your marketing plan at least every quarter on your calendar, if not more frequently.

The more you do, the more you will see the results and magic. You will also learn what works and what does not work for your business through practical experience in doing them, and your future events will become better and better.

Final Suggestions on Events

Whenever you hold an event, it is suggested you keep a written record of some kind. The best way to do this is to keep a log book. A log book become useful in the long term for the small business marketer, as one can refer back to it and repeat what work. One can also use it as a way to recall all the important details of what went into the planning and preparation.

Therefore in keeping a log, it is always better to record as much detail about the preparation, planning and what the outcome was as possible. It is better to keep this log record as you go along in preparing for the event, and to make notes immediately following the conclusion of the event while details are fresh in your mind. Make notes of not only what you did to prepare for it, but what attendance you received, how the public responded, how long it went, what the weather conditions were, etc.

All of these details can be important to have recorded when doing multiple events and re-visiting them several months or even a year or two down the road. It becomes easy to repeat exactly what worked in the past when one has a record of what happened.

Written records of events will also help when one discovers later on that word of mouth is driving people into the store or business. The sales manager can train the salespeople to listen for the word of mouth referral by asking the question: *'how did you find out about us?'* somewhere in the sales presentation. If it was word of mouth, you will certainly learn this from this simple question.

Researching the word of mouth can be another way to boost discovery for future events. You may learn from word of mouth that a certain aspect or feature of the event was most memorable to the people that attended, and that was what promoted them to tell others. Finding this out, it becomes very easy to repeat this in the future.

Keeping a log book on what was done can also aid you in sorting out what the people were talking about weeks, months or even years later. Having a written record of the history of all past events including what happened, how it went and its overall form can help with repeating the best of the best of your brilliant events in the future.

SECRET #8

Rotating, Changing & Adjusting Signs & Displays

If may seem unusual to include this as a basic secret of small business sales management success. What does the rotation of signs and displays have to do with sales or business?

This particular point will apply to any small business that operates from a store front or showroom, and relies on any part of their business from this environment. However, some of the principles that will be discussed here could also apply to an online storefront as well.

Signage

Signage is defined as: Graphic designs, words, messages, symbols or emblems used to identify or direct, call attention to or give warning in the exchange of information.

Signs are used in business for many purposes to help sell products. They can serve as messages or news about the product or services you are offering. They can describe details about the product or service. Signs can also direct someone to buy a product or service, or in some cases to not buy. They call attention to where things are in the place of business, as well as identify what items are on sale or discounted.

Signs can have many uses. However, the primary use in sales is to *capture attention.* This capturing of attention can be to direct the customer to do something, so somewhere or just give them enough information to peak their interest to involve a salesperson.

A sign that stays in one location for too long can become part of the scenery and ignored. This is true for signs with the same message day after day. Once a customer reads the sign, they tend to file the message away and ignore it even if they pass that same sign every day.

Signage is important as they can serve as a sort of bait to draw a customer into a place of business. They can also serve as a source of information to answer customers questions when there is no one there to speak with, such as during a time when the business is crowded and busy with other customers, or after hours when the store is closed and all that is visible are the signs in the windows.

To be able to see the importance of rotating or adjusting signs is to think beyond the present customer in front of you today. It is thinking about the customer that is not present, or will come to see your store tomorrow or the day after. It means sending a message to a customer who perhaps came to the store before and did not quite get see the sign or get the message.

Moving signs around can spark new action when least expected. Changing the message or direction from time to time can add new life to stagnant flows of customers on sales.

Signs help to create a flow of traffic in a place of business, as well as compel purchasing in a subtle way. They can also become ignored after a time by customers who frequent your business on a regular basis. Therefore it is a successful activity to update the signs from time to time, as well as move them around.

Here is a list of tips for adjusting signage:

➢ Move the sign to a new location entirely
➢ Move a sign to a higher or lower position
➢ Move the sign to the right or left of where it was previously, and change the direction of the arrow if there is one
➢ Change the sign to a different color, but leave the same message
➢ Change the message in the sign
➢ Change the type of sign materiel (i.e. paper, wood, plastic, etc.)
➢ Add balloons to a sign
➢ Add ribbons to a sign
➢ Turn the sign upside down
➢ Turn the sign to an odd angle

- ➤ Hang the sign from a string so it has motion
- ➤ Shine a spotlight on the sign at night
- ➤ Add a second sign that is attached to the first one with additional information
- ➤ Have a person or costumed character hold the sign
- ➤ Change signs and displays to match the holiday or season
- ➤ Add some humor to a sign or display

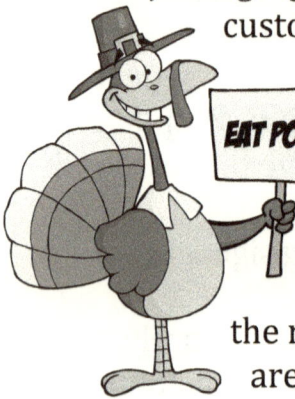

Adjusting signs in creative ways can help to keep customers looking at them and reading the messages. The object of a sign is the deliver the message to the person who reads it. The secondary objective is the repeat the message over and over again so that the person acts upon the message. Having a system where you are adjusting the signs on a regular basis can help to draw continual attention to the message intended to deliver.

How frequently should you adjust signage?

If you are running a business with a lot of traffic, and people coming through that are repeat customers, then signs should be adjusted at a minimum daily. More is better in that situation. If your business is moderate to light body traffic, then you might be looking at a weekly or bi-weekly adjustment plan. The real test to take into consideration to determine how often to adjust them is: *when was the last time someone responded to that sign?*

If you are getting zero sales after having made regular sales on an item with a sign on it previously, then that might be a good indicator to change or adjust the sign. Another important point to consider is whether the sign in question is an internal sign or an outward facing sign targeting people who drive or walk past the business.

There is also a reverse rule to take into consideration with this concept of adjusting signs as well. The reverse rule would be: *if a sign is working and people are responding to it with sales, then do not change it.*

Essentially, whenever you have a working sign do not change it or adjust it until it stops working for you. When sales dry up where a sign is posted, make a change. This is where it becomes very important to observe and make note of what signs are working, and which ones are not. Working signs do not require adjustment or change. Non-working ones do. It is that simple.

Displays

Displays differ from signs in that they are typically a feature of the product or service. They can be stacks or shelves of the product one is selling, or any such combination. Displays can also be hung on a wall, stacked on a podium or arranged in some sort of mechanical showcase to draw attention to it.

Displays, much like signs follow the same basic principle. They require monitoring for activity and sales of the product from the display, and also adjustments when they cease to capture a sale.

One of the best ways to spark new life into a showroom that features displays of the product one is selling is to do a rotation of them all on a regular scheduled basis. Making displays too permanent can act as a detriment to a sales manager.

To understand this, one must examine the purpose of displays. What is it? What is the purpose of a display of a product or service? *It is to capture interest from a prospective customer or repeat customers.* That is the bare bones purpose of any display of products or services.

Therefore when one understands this purpose, the one can easily see that rotating or changing displays on a regular basis helps to create interest. Whenever a customer has been in your store before, they see they displays. When you make changes, they have to look again.

Some business owners slip into an operating basis of only changing displays when they have new inventory. This can work for some businesses that have new inventory every week, but with many small businesses this is not always the case. Also, what about existing inventory? On must consider adjusting displays for existing inventory if it is not selling.

I will give you an example. I used to own a stained glass business in the Atlanta, Georgia metro area. At one point we decided to begin selling pre-made stained glass Tiffany style lamps in our showroom as accessory items to our custom doors and windows. It also opened up a new clientele for us who may not be able to purchase our larger more expensive items, but they could bring some stained glass into their home with a lamp or other light fixture.

We learned that when a new item was displayed, it would draw attention for about 1-2 weeks from our regular customers and then if it did not sell by then, it would sit there for months. However, when we simply moved this existing inventory around the showroom to a new location, it would sell. Upon discovery of this, we put in a regular rotation of all lamps and lighting displays every 1-2 weeks.

We would concentrate on moving lamps around that were not selling or had been with us awhile. Whenever we did this, we would experience a fresh batch of new sales over the coming days and weeks. Often lamps would sell that had been there in the store for months, but now that they were in the right display location to enhance its appearance to a customer, it sold.

This discovery brought about a new awareness of the importance of moving display items around a showroom floor. These methods helped to sell off stagnant inventory, and make way for new inventory. It helped also to give our showroom the appearance of constant change in the mind of the prospective customers, and the interest we created boosted our traffic tremendously.

Here is a list of tips that we learned about moving and rotating displays that worked to help sell existing inventory when it was not selling:

> Move the display item to a new location in the showroom
> Change the lighting on a display item
> Change the height on how something is displayed, either higher or lower than it was before.
> Change the direction the item is displayed
> Change the color of the pedestal or table the item sits upon
> Change the angle of how something is displayed
> Change the window the item is featured in to a new window or position in the showroom
> Hang the item from the ceiling
> Place the item on the floor in front of other displays
> Hide the item in the backroom for a week, and then bring it out again to a new location in the showroom

- Change the type of background the item it displayed in front of
- Change the type of pedestal or table display the item is sitting on
- Change the color or darkness or lightness of a pedestal or table an item is sitting on
- Pair up the item with a similar item
- Pair up the item with a different item
- Pair up the item with the same type of item
- Place the item next to a larger or smaller item of the same style
- Place the item next to a completely dissimilar item
- Add a sign to the item
- Add a smaller or larger sign
- Change the location of the sign on the item or color
- Change the price tag to a new larger or smaller price tag
- Draw a red line through a higher price on the price tag, and hand write in a new lower price
- Place a moving item near a display, such as a flashing, blinking or moving light, fan, balloon or ribbon
- Make sure the displays are lit up at night and visible through the store windows for night time window shoppers
- Set up timers on evening lighting to turn off and on at peak hours after the store is closed
- Use neon or other creative lighting around a display

> ➤ If displaying multiple items of a kind on a shelf or other display, remove one and leave a noticeable black space giving the impression someone already bought one, therefore the customer seeing this should too.

If you use your imagination with your displays, you can see there are many ways to be creative in rotating or changing them to create the illusion to the customer that your inventory is fresh and constantly changing, even if it is not. The use of displays rotation can help boost sales for any small business, and it is quite often overlooked as to how important this is.

Showrooms or businesses that do not change displays take on the appearance in the mind of a consumer that the business is stagnant and not changing. If they walk in and see the same item in the same location they saw the last time they walked in, it communicates instantly to them that the item is not selling. It can even put a doubt in their minds as to whether they want to buy it themselves, simply because no one else has before them.

So it is really a psychological game one is playing with the mind of the customer with regards to rotating, moving and changing displays around:

> ➤ One is making them look around again and get their bearings.

➤ One is testing their recall on what items you had in the store the last time they were there, and they often remember items based on locations they tagged the item within their mind.

➤ One is compelling them to take a fresh look at all of your items, new and old on display, and examine and consider them once again.

➤ It also makes a customer dispel old ideas they may have placed on a display that caused them to not consider purchasing an item the last time they saw it, and it may make them reconsider it again in a new unit of time.

➤ It inspires the customer to conclude that your store is alive with 'change' and your products are in demand because they are constantly moving and changing.

➤ In this way it gives credibility to the business through this illusion of demand others have for your products simply because a customer cannot possibly remember all the items you had on display before, and therefore will conclude that your inventory is turning over and over.

Over time customers who frequent the store or showroom will tell others about your business, and simply by the created illusion of an ever-changing inventory, they will tell others about how successful your store is. They will also tell others to buy items they like when they see them, or they might not be there the next time.

Summary on Signs & Displays

When one understands that signage and displays are best used as a transitional and adjustable tool for sales, then there is a lot of magic that follows.

The major result is that one can feel more in control of the flow of customer dollars into ones place of business. One can do something about slow traffic by getting all the sales staff and employees to get involved in moving displays about the showroom or display room, including window displays and keep the place looking alive with the appearance of new products in the mind of the consumer.

SECRET #9

Staying Connected & Working Old Leads Again & Again

The magical tool of success to running any small business is to never lose track of your customers, and stay connected. This can mean even staying connected over weeks, months or years between selling them your products or services. It becomes a tool of marketing for the business to develop a system that does this.

The biggest successful action for a small business marketer is to have a system in place in their regular course of operation that enables them to practice identity capturing.

What is identity capturing?

It is the collecting of your customer's names, addresses and phone numbers who buy from you and also in this modern day *their email addresses!* It also includes capturing the identities of people who visited your store, and even ones that did not buy. *What do you know about these people?* They have some kind of interest in your business! They at least know where your business is, and could be prompted to return as well.

Many small businesses exist exclusively on point of purchase sales from their store, and do not even think to capture names of the people who buy from them. *Why is capturing these names important?* Essentially, this is important because it provides you with a resource to reach out to them again in the future. It gives you a chance to sell them more products and services. Your best customer and easiest one to sell is *the one whom has already made a purchase from you!*

Using a system of capturing identities enables you to work a system where you can build relationships with former clients, and create more sales. Therefore, identity capturing requires also the additional step of following up with them for future purchases.

Essentially this really becomes a two part process. *Capturing the identity and creating a system that enables you to follow up.* So let's explore both of these points in detail.

Identity Capturing

What are the best ways to capture your buyer's identity? To begin, if you are going to do this directly face to face with the public, you will have to have a storefront or even a booth at a public trade show or other public show like a local festival. To take on such an activity, must be able and willing to talk to people, and engage them in conversation to a greater or lesser degree. Identity capturing is not something that one successfully accomplishes by placing it on automatic. You have to be willing to talk to people, and encourage them to give you their information.

The first two things you have to ask yourself is:

1. *How valuable a list of names would be to you that consisted entirely customers that had made a purchase from you or were familiar with your work?*

2. *What price would you put on a list of 100, 200 or even 500 names of those types of people?*

While you are considering the answer to those questions, let's examine some methods to capture people's identities at a trade show or home show, as these types of shows are common in a community and offer booths that can give a local small business some additional exposure over a one to three day period.

The fish bowl giveaway

The easiest way to start with identity capturing is to place a bowl on your table that allows people to place their business card or contact information written on a piece of paper into it. The draw for them doing this is usually best done with some sort of giveaway item, usually one of the more desirable items in your booth.

In order for this to work, the giveaway item has to be something people want, so you will want to giveaway an item that is one of your most popular pieces and in high demand. It can also be a popular item in the marketplace like an iPad, camera or some other popular item with the demographic you are seeking to capture identities from.

To encourage them to enter into this contest and give you the information you desire, inform them that the winner will be notified through phone or email, so make sure they also include that on their slip of paper or business card.

If you do this throughout the show, you will capture names and identities of a lot of people who are your prospective customers and people who have just seen your booth who become your future prospects.

The value of this second group of people is that they attended that show and have an interest in something related to the show, so they could become a future customer for you at a later show if you stay in touch.

One cannot stay in touch if you do not have their contact information to do so, so try a giveaway to capture it!

The sign-up sheet

This can be a simple pad of paper that you keep on the table and ask people who purchased or engaged you in conversation to sign up on. This can even be prospects that did not buy for whatever reason, but you still encourage them to sign up for a giveaway contest you are doing or just to *'sign up for our newsletter to find out about our next shows'* or *'get the latest news happening with our store'*.

Asking prospects and customers to *'sign up for a newsletter'* works for businesses that have such a unique product that they literally have fans who are in awe of their work, and may buy more again in the future.

This second approach to *'sign up for a newsletter'* may not work as well for booths built around smaller impulse buy items, so in that case I would recommend doing the giveaway to capture names as an alternative.

Important tip: When you provide any sign-up sheet, always write a bogus name in the first line with a name, address, phone number and email address. For some reason, people will commonly avoid being the first to sign such a list, but will willingly sign if others have done so. I suppose it appears safe to do so if others have done it before them.

The guest book

This is similar to the basic sign-up sheet, but a little more of a formal approach. This is where you buy one of those professional guest books used at weddings or other special occasions, and have it sitting on an easel inside your booth or near the entrance of your store where people who visit can sign up their names. You can tie this in with a giveaway of an item or free service if you wish. This approach is a classy way of saying *'give me your name and contact info'* and works well for the specialty artists who create larger more expensive works.

Important tip: When you provide any guest book, always write a fake name in the first line of a blank sheet with a name, address, phone number and email address. Just like the basic sign-up sheet, people will commonly avoid being the first to sign such a list, but will willingly sign if others have done so before them.

Live Internet sign-up

If you are at a show where you have electric power and can arrange internet access, you can also set up a sign-up form where people can sit down and take a survey or enter a contest by filling out information right in your booth online or in your place of business, and this captures their identity. You do not often see this at outdoor shows because indoor shows offer a setting where this is easier to do. However, as long as you have electricity and a climate where people are willing to sit down and take the survey or sign up, it can work anywhere.

It is not a common practice now, but it is a practice done at a lot of professional trade shows and so I thought I would include this here for those businesses that are also computer savvy and interested in trying this approach. A paperless lead capturing approach right in your store or show booth and it can save a lot of time.

If you set something like this up, it works best to have several computers or another means for paper lead capturing that you are using as well, as people can be slow in entering info on a computer and when there are a lot of people doing this you do not want to lose potential leads.

The nudge

If you have the luxury of having a few extra volunteers helping you with your trade show booth or at your place of business, it is always a good idea to assign at least one or two of them the task of identity capturing by having them man the station where you have a sign-up form or drawing, and have them nudge people to enter.

I have found that setting up a contest bowl or offering any kind of sign-up sheet does not mean that people will automatically enter their name; in fact most will not do so unless prompted. My best advice is to have someone who is the most dynamic or 'willing to talk to people' personality to be responsible for this job at your booth. Using the salespeople in training is a good way for them to get used to interacting with customers and learning what questions the customers will ask in a non-formal setting.

At professional trade shows, they usually select the prettiest young girl, or handsome young man to perform this role. If you do not have such a person helping you, that is okay. If available, select a young child who is cute and willing to talk to people or anyone who is can be irresistible to people so they will not say no. Simply choose anyone who is friendly and personable. Most anyone can become good at this role if one practices. It takes the willingness to charm people, flatter them, tease them, be overtly friendly to them and repeatedly ask people to sign-up all throughout the show.

I have seen some show exhibitors use a costumed character to perform this duty of asking for sign-ups. If it is a full body costumed suit, often the person wearing it does not have to do anything other than gesture to the sign up book, bowl or list and act like a character. You can get away with a lot as a costumed character, and it is a great draw for kids. People love to have their picture taken with a costumed character.

The person wearing the costumed suit should give out high-fives, hugs and basically be larger than life without getting too caught up in the role to forget the sign-up sheet, book or contest. Doing the costumed character stunt works best on cooler days if outdoors, and events that are not likely to get someone caught in the rain. Doing this on a hot July day at an outdoor show can really limit a person's time in a full body costume, as they can get quite warm and it is akin to walking around with a sleeping bag all over your body, even if they are ventilated and have a built-in fan. A better costume for a hot day is to dress like a clown, pirate or some other character that does not require a full body suit. Indoors shows however typically are air conditioned and climate controlled, so this is not usually a problem.

Online Identity Capturing

Identity capturing can also be done online through social media pages, website forums and getting people to sign up for an email newsletter on the company website. There are many ways to venture into identity capturing online, and the identities of people can be organized in a contact manager which we will discuss later in this chapter.

Creativity is the magic

One can get creative as one would wish with identity capturing, and there certainly can be many ways to do this. What you are trying to obtain is the customer or prospects name, phone number, address and email address.

Quite honestly if you can at least get a name and email address, you can turn these lists into a gold mine for future business for the company. If you find it too complicated or slow to ask for all of their contact info, one should then simply focus on going for just the name and email. With those two basic pieces of information you can do a lot with future promotions.

Follow Up

The value and return from the efforts of identity capturing comes from having a system in place for follow up. There are many ways to do this, and any business should have at least some system in place for contacting people again.

Now let's examine some of the various ways to do this from the very simple, to the more automated and sophisticated. All are easy to do, if you are willing to take the time to stay organized with it. It is well worth the advantage and return from sales.

The very simple, non-computer method

Some business marketers are not computer savvy at all, and need a basic system to be able to contact their former customers and prospects without using a computer. Today, there are some very simple ways to do this with just keeping paper records.

The easiest and least technically complicated way will require that you at least own or have access to a copy machine, and know how to use one. You can purchase brands of mailing labels (example: Avery labels), and in those boxes of labels there is usually a black and white template of which you can make copies of and use to hand write in or type with a typewriter the names and addresses of the identities you have captured.

From this you can build a master list, and one that you can make copies of using the mailing labels and have a means to mail these people information about your business. Keep hand writing or typing onto your list and expand your files on each and every show, and keep these as your master list. Whenever you want to send out a mailing, you can simply use a copy machine and copy these names onto labels and peel off and attach these printed labels to your mailing.

If you want to send out a newsletter or postcard to let people know about your next show, you can coordinate with a local printing company to make these items for you or hand draw them out yourself and use your copy machine to print them onto postcard stock paper. Then cut them into postcards or fold them into newsletter and mail them with postage attached.

This is perhaps the most basic approach for those who are not familiar with computers, but certainly not the most cost effective one. Paper, printing and postage mailing can be more expensive over time to use for this style of marketing, and due to cost can mean that you cannot afford to do this frequently.

However, it is it a very non-technical way to go about it, and is better than having no system in place.

Computer lead capturing methods

If you have some basic working knowledge of how to use a home computer or the internet, there are a lot of ways to manage your lists and make contacting your people very easy.

The first would be to get a copy of the program Excel from Microsoft, and learn to use it. You can set up a template and manually enter names into a master list and use this list to export them to a mailing label format and print mailers as needed. There are also several other lead management software services you can sign up for online that will enable you to do this as well, and here are a few you can explore:

www.constantcontact.com
www.printmanager.com
www.freelancetech.com

The next and perhaps the most low cost and easiest way to manage leads and stay in contact is to exclusively focus on names and email addresses, and send out email newsletters and reminders of upcoming shows.

This is best done in coordination with having your own website too, that way you can put your website on all of your contact information and people who you miss capturing as an identity can perhaps visit your website later on in the privacy of their own home, and sign up for your newsletter if they wish.

Once you have a website set up, you will want to sign up or a separate service that allows you to manage email list and create your own newsletters. If you search on the internet, you can find several companies that provide you with this service. They provide you with a link or 'widget' once you set up your account with them that you can add to your website and capture leads and identities from there, but also enable you to enter names onto your list that you captured from your shows and manage your lists.

The email management service I recommend because it is user friendly is: *mailchimp.com*, because they enable you to tag your lists into groups, which can work great for you to email former customers if you group them into shows you attended. When you return to that show, you can send out an advanced email and remind them to come see you again.

Mailchimp.com is entirely free up to lists of 2000 and then they begin to charge you a low monthly rate for the service. A mailing list of 2000 would be quite an achievement for an arts and crafts show vendor artist, and it one is using a list that large, certainly one is making money with it and can afford the additional fees. Until you reach that size, it is an awesome way to stay organized for free.

Using your identities captured with awesome follow up tricks

Newsletters: Services like mailchimp.com have platforms where one can create a newsletter, and custom sign up forms that you can add to your website. A newsletter can be created months ahead of time, and set up to automatically be sent to your list on specified dates. Your mailing list can be working for you by means of pre-set automated advanced emails even when your business is closed.

While at shows: When you have names from a show that your business is at, you may want to enter them into your mailing database after each show. This way you can constantly build upon a master and even sub-lists and stay organized with it. With online access, you can even go back to your hotel room or your home base the evenings you are at an overnight show and enter the identities you collected that day. Send all of your daily visitors an exclusive coupon for the next day, and see if you can get them back for additional purchases.

Coupons: With any identity collection and follow up program, always think with rewarding everyone who signs up. Make them all winners by giving them a coupon to use for a discount on your website, or at your place of business. Invite them to give this coupon to their friends, and email it to them.

Advanced reminders: Once you have collected names, you can email people in advance letting them know the next trade, business or other type of show you are going to be at. At first you can email your entire list, and keep them all notified. If you are traveling around and doing several shows, you might want to sort out the names by the show, region or State you captured it in and send out advanced emails to your 'Georgia' or 'Florida' customers for example. Once a list grows, you can selectively mail reminders to groups by staying organized with mailing list management software.

You can even used advanced reminders to tell customers about upcoming sales, promotions or specials at you place of business. You can send reminders about back to school or the holiday shopping too.

Summary on Follow-Up

When one is looking at the subject of identity capturing and follow up, there are systems for every small business marketer depending on what they are willing to do.

The most important thing to remember is that identity capturing is important, and even if you do not have a computer, or the time to learn. Then all identities should have a system in place to follow up. One should have at least a basic system working that you expand on later or hire someone to manage for you. The best system to have is one that works for you. Any system is better than no system.

So how much is a list of customer names and prospects that have seen your product to you? If you read this chapter, you are probably realizing the income potential from such a list. What has been presented here is a low cost way for you to obtain the information.

Certainly one has the expense of the item one is giving away, and the costs involved in setting up follow up systems, but the return on this investment into the future can be huge. Having a point of purchase system online that is connected to your business website can help you make sales 24 hours a day, 7 days a week. They can also drive customers into your business location.

Essentially the more information you can gather, the more you can use. If you can get birthdays for example, you can send them a card with coupon for through birthday. There are even companies that make this very easy to keep track of to do this, such as: *www.sendoutcards.com*.

Whatever your plan is, make sure it includes capturing identities and contacting them over and over again. This is the way you use the power of where your sales have been before, and take sales quotas to new heights as you expand the customer base by working all your leads new and old alike.

SECRET #10

Sales Meetings with Results

One of the best secrets for any small business and sales manager is having the sales staff working together as a team. Sales meetings are an integral part of any business that relies on the production of salespeople to sell the company's products and services. What is the best way to conduct a sales meeting? What is the real benefit of such a meeting?

The Benefits of Sales Meetings

It really becomes a question of do you want a sales group or a sales team? A mere group can exist, and have some success and also may never truly succeed. A team plays together, and plays to win. There is a distinguishing difference. One is adrift, with the hopes that it will get somewhere by chance, and the other is driven as a unified determined unit towards the goal post of success.

Groups drift with the tide, and sometimes make landfall and achieve success. Teams not only make landfall repeatedly, they establish ferries and build bridges to get there faster and more efficiently, over and over again.

The occupation of a salesperson can be a very lonely job, especially if you are involved in exclusively outside sales, and not operating out of a showroom or office environment. It is difficult to learn new information strictly on your own, and some people do not make it because of this.

A group of outside sales people can quickly become a random, disjointed scattering of people, if not organized and pooled together once in awhile to bring them all on the same page. Even working as apparent individuals, they still can be brought together as a team. In today's smart phone and Internet era, this is not only possible, but a reality with any creative sales manager.

One of the most valuable tools for a sales manager to use to develop a cohesive functioning sales team is the *sales meeting*. I have worked as a salesperson in several different companies over the years, and there are some sales managers that I worked for that never held meetings, and some that held meetings only a few times a year. Certainly with certain types of sales teams, it is not always possible to meet in the same location every week, but today's Internet resource makes it possible for everyone at least to come together online.

Website platforms like: *GoToMeeting.com* is just one example, and there are many others available online. Every salesperson simply logs in at an agreed upon time, wherever they are on the road, and plugs in an earpiece and attends a meeting complete with power point images, video and instruction organized and run by the sales manager.

When I began as a sales manager in the early 1990's in my own business, I originally followed the pattern of not holding meetings like so many other companies I had witnessed. We would do quick briefings now and then, and a lot of one on one instruction as needed.

I found on some subjects, I was doing a lot of repeating of things, over and over. I was also not remembering what information I had given to which salesperson, and tried to flank this practice through memos, etc. This created inconsistency in trying to get them to function as a team.

It was only when I finally implemented sales meetings that I saw the magic in them, as well as the results. I soon discovered that if I wanted *consistency* in sales as a team, instead of a group, I needed to put in *weekly* sales meetings in order to make the *group* into a *team*. Weekly sales meetings became the established success with my team, but this is only half of the solution that made it successful. The other half was the format.

There are many approaches to how a manager of sales people can conduct a sales meeting. Quite often with a lot of companies I have been a part of the pattern consists of 90-100% of the meeting with the sales manager giving weekly reports on sales, and maybe some news on product changes, or prices, and not much else. This information is important, and has its place in such a meeting, as it is important news they need to have. However, I never much cared for this as the sole body of content.

My approach was much more interactive. When I established my weekly sales meetings, I introduced sharing of ideas between sales people, training, and creative thinking practices to each meeting. This consisted of 90-95% of the meeting, and 5-10% was regulated to news of product updates, prices, specials, etc.

I always assumed the viewpoint that the purpose of sales meetings were not to pound in the heads of sales people the company mantra, but to educate, share wisdom and make them better, as well as inspire them to become super sales people. They became *sales training and inspiration meetings*. If I could achieve this feeling when they left a meeting, then at least the day it was held would be successful for everyone, and perhaps even the week that followed.

A typical meeting consisted of the following outline in terms of format:

- *Announcing the start of the meeting*
- *Introductions (if there are new members of the team)*
- *Interactive discussions on the objections or problems experienced that week*
- *New sales tool discussed/drilled/training*
- *Creative thinking*
- *Successes*
- *News and updates*
- *End of meeting*

This was the general flow of the meeting week after week. Sometimes one step would be so engaging that it became the bulk of the meeting. I was always willing to keep it flexible. What I was looking to do was inspire and gets the wheels of creativity flowing every week, to keep the team engaged in selling with enthusiasm every day.

I learned from these meetings what they were running into individually, and as a group. Together we often worked out the resolution to major problems in selling the product that I would have otherwise never known was happening. Sometimes the troubles they ran into were so subtle, that you would never have encountered it outside of a meeting as a manager.

However, when the small matter came up in open discussion, it would become clear how it was impacting the sales presentations of the entire group. As a sales manager, the meetings became where I was too able to learn, and thereby improve the situation for the team members by fixing the problem, making adjustments to marketing or even directing the serious matters to the owner's attention, and so forth.

Most of the meetings were between 30 minutes to and hour at most. I came prepared for the meeting every week, as I was the director. Each week the sales team members also knew they could bring forward issues as well, so they too came prepared.

Now I would like to go into each of these areas of the meeting further so you can get a better feel for how they worked.

Start & End of the Meeting

I always started precisely on time, and announced it loudly. I soon learned that attendance and punctuality did not become an issue, because the sales people that were late missed out on the treasures of information that gave their other fellow sales people the edge. The meetings were diamonds and gold nuggets of information, and if you were too unorganized and were late, then you short changed yourself. I made sure they all knew it.

If you really want to gain 100% attendance, make any bonus you offer that coming week have a qualifying requirement of being at role call at the meetings when they start. Next week you will see a full house ten minutes early.

However, for the most part the sales people who are serious about succeeding will be there, and on time, the others won't be around long anyway as they lack the drive to really make it in the profession. So concentrate on the ones who show up for meetings and make them better.

In addition to starting on time, I always tried to end on time. Sometimes it was hard to contain the enthusiasm of the attendees, and they wanted to continue longer, so in those cases I would survey those in attendance and see if they all agreed to extend another 15 minutes.

However, most of the time we held our meeting an hour before the store opened, and once that time came, the phones were ringing and customers were coming in, so there was no room to extend. In most cases, if more information needed to be addressed, I would take note and take it up at the next meeting.

Introductions

I always took a moment to introduce new sales people, and had everyone in the group go around the room and introduce themselves to them. This, for obvious reasons, helps the new person feel like they belong and are accepted.

It helps with participation from them, although not only at the first meeting. Usually at the first few meetings they are doing mostly a lot of listening, but by the third meeting I begin to insist they participate.

If you allow a new sales person to be a bystander too long, they will remain individuated from the group, which is not what you want when building a team.

Interactive discussions on the objections or problems experienced that week

This was where the meeting really became interesting. The first ten to fifteen minutes usually of every meeting I would ask those in attendance to share an experience from the prior week with a customer or prospect that they dealt with where they had ran into trouble.

Either they could not handle the objection the customer had for buying, or experienced a problem they could not overcome for the customer, or they lost a deal to a competitor because they could not keep the customer engaged and close them in some way. These situations would be pulled out by me if they were not volunteered. If I had knowledge of a salesperson losing a sale, and it was not volunteered, I would ask 'What happened with that customer named John Smith this week?'

At that point the salesperson would relay the story of how their presentation went, the questions that were asked, and how they responded, etc. (You do not want to do this with new people at their first or second meeting, just ones that have been around awhile).

What you are trying to do is create a forum for salespeople to talk, share their experiences, and hear other approaches from other sales people on how they would have handled that situation. It has to become safe for them to discuss their failures for them to dissect the experience and learn from it. Most of the time they learn different viewpoints and approaches that could have been taken, as shared by other sales people present.

This becomes an educational experience for not only the person who lost a sale, but for others who are there taking it all in. I would try to cover anywhere from 2-5 examples in a given meeting and offer alternative approaches to them in the group setting of what they could have done, or do in the future. I would also ask other sales people to discuss if they had experienced this same scenario, and how they had resolved it successfully. This kind of discussion can run too long if you let it, so you will want to develop a report of getting to the facts quickly, so as to be able to cover as much ground as time permits with this portion of the meeting.

What is most important to understand about this group discussion is that I *never* made anyone wrong for failing at a sale or losing one. It was always targeted at being an analytical discussion among professionals, so emotions were cast to the side. What was most important was that the salespeople present learned from the experience, and learned new approaches to help them succeed when faced with the same scenario again in the future.

Therefore this part of the meeting became an interactive learning experience for them and an invaluable resource for all salespeople new and old alike. We took up the topic of failed sales closes and approached it as a science, rather than a point of making anyone feel bad. In this part of the meeting, we learned immediately what the competition was saying to our customers, as invariably some salesperson would lose a sale due to this tactic being used against them.

By airing the experience for all to hear, we were able to dissect the experience and share wisdom. If no one had experienced this situation before, we opened discussion on hypothetical solutions on how it could be handled in the future, and these were then tried and reports were made the next meeting on how they worked. Whenever a new customer objection for buying was discovered, it became a discussion surrounding the revelation 'How interesting is that?' and like explorers discovering a new life form on a planet of sales ideas, we pulled out our magnifying glasses and closed in as a team to learn more about it.

By using this approach in our sales meetings, my sales team learned new closing tools every week, and rebuttals to common customer objections for not buying. They evolved into a group of incredibly effective sales people. Closing ratios fell from a 1 out of 10 (1/10) average to a 1/3 or in many of the more experienced sales people 1/2.

It got to a point where at this section of the weekly meeting it became hard to find sales each week *that did not close.* However, we would still dig for them and air them. If there were none, we would take up the ones that did close, but did not go so smoothly. Then the discussion became about: *what could they have done* to make the process smoother and faster.

In other words, in this part of the meeting we addressed in order the following topics:

A) Failed closes
B) Rough sales
C) Slow sales

You will find there is no limit to the experiences that can be exposed, examined and dissected as well as learned by one and all in this part of the meeting. There never seemed to be an end, and all who attended found new nuggets of wisdom each time from this short section of the meeting each and every week.

New sales tool discussed/drilled/training

This is the part of the meeting that required advanced preparation on my part as a sales manager. Though out the week I would study sales material, books, lectures, and any other published work I could find that offered useful tools, wisdom and different perspective on the sales approach.

I would take up one piece of information each week, and present it to the group. I would read it to the group, or play a short taped lecture. Usually it was not more than a few paragraphs of information, or minutes from a lecture. I would present it, and re-read or re-play the material as needed a few times, and then I would present how this could be applied to our business. Then I would open up discussion on what their feedback and viewpoint is on how they could apply this material, have they experienced anything like the author or speaker was discussing, etc.

Sometimes we would take the material, and face across from each other and role play the lesson until we gained some comfort with using it. Then the marching orders to the group were to apply that material in the next coming week, and bring feedback to the next meeting. In this way they were always getting new material to experiment with, as well as learning tried and proven techniques that they were excited about.

What is important to note is that I would never during this part of the meeting try to present something *too lengthy* as one would lose their attention. I preferred the gems or wisdom that I could find that was one to four lines long from some sales text of lecture. I learned that I achieved greater application if I took the approach of spoon feeding them nuggets of wisdom, than trying to present huge amounts of data in a short amount of time.

Short amounts of data allowed me to go over it again and again, and drill it home through repetition and discussion, and the materiel was able to be put into use rather than something we covered and they forgot about. It is much easier to take a short datum and repeat it ten times, over and over, clarifying it more each time, than to take one long two page subject and read it once. I was more likely to see the bright candles of understanding be lit from a short gem of wisdom from this approach, and I had accomplished what I intended, which was to give them a new tool for their arsenal to use with customers.

This of course all depends on the datum itself, and how useful it is to the salesperson, but I learned there is a separate art to this as well to be able to seek out interesting nuggets to share. The more you do it, the better you will get, especially the more you get to know your team.

Not every tool was used each and every week. Some of the gems of wisdom I presented would perhaps be used in only one out of fifty customers, so the next week may only yield one or two stories from someone who used the tool that week. It did not matter to me as much that it was used right away, but more so that they understood it, adopted it and had it to use in the future.

Sometimes during this part of the meeting, I would have them do a group practical exercise instead of learning a new tool. I would tell them I needed 100 ways to describe one aspect of the doors we were selling on the floor. They would start calling out 'mahogany', 'beautiful grain', 'hardwood', 'beautiful', 'solid', etc. I had a large grease board and was writing them all down as they said them. I wanted them to be able to churn these descriptions out like second nature when talking to people about the product.

This kind of practical exercises worked tremendously well, and it also got them contributing together as a team in the most creative circus one would ever witness. Exercises like this became something they also looked forward to. Additionally, it gave all present new descriptive adjectives to use in their vocabulary for describing the product to customers. This then became an interactive learning experience on its own, where they created their own nuggets on the fly, and shared them spontaneously with each other.

Creative Thinking

At this part of the meeting I opened discussion for new creative ideas that someone came up with and thought it should be known about. Sometimes it was a suggestion for a new sale, or a product package. Sometimes it was a new product they would like us to try to acquire, or presentation material of some kind they would like the company to develop. Other times it was a new presentation that someone had been working on and wanted to share.

If it was something that could be presented to the group, I let them, giving them a time limit. If there were suggestions for new sales packages, products or promotional material, I wrote them down and checked into these for the coming week and reported the findings or outcome in the next week company news part of the meeting.

Over the years, this part of the meeting became an invaluable resource for ideas to improve the company product lines and promotional materials. I will give you a few examples on how this became profitable for the entire group:

Example 1: We had a showroom building where the sales staff worked. There were models of doors and windows on display in two showroom areas, and there were two design office rooms where the staff sat down with clients and finalized sales. In the front showroom there were these very high ceilings like a gallery, and for so many years we had displays on the lower walls and nothing above.

At one of the meetings a proposal was made to have posters made of some of our best selling front entry door packages, frame them and place them up high on the walls all around the room. As ridiculously simple as this may seem, the idea had never occurred to me or the other owners of the company to use this space for anything.

So within a few weeks we had posters made, framed and put on these walls. The impact was tremendous. Not only did it increase sales, but we were selling the same door packages more frequently and this cut down custom design costs in production as the designs were repeated, and as a result we saw a slight increase in profit too.

Example 2: In the beginning years of our business, and the first few years of our showroom, we focused on selling exclusively our own custom doors and windows. Then in one meeting, someone brought up the situation that we are losing customers who walk in each and every week, and see nothing below $800 and are walking out. They are out in the area shopping, and if they are not in the market for a front entryway or window for their home, they are coming in, looking around, and leaving without spending any money. The argument presented made sense. 'Why not get something in the showroom that they could buy and my salespeople could sell to them?'

So a creative discussion was engaged in on the subject of products we could buy and introduce as retail items. After some months of research and trial and experimentation, our company introduced stained glass lamps, mirrors, and other smaller glass related gift items. This became so popular, that in the month of December every year following, driven by holiday shopping sales before Christmas, we began selling more lamps than the gross income from our regular custom windows and doors. It also boosted the company's gross income by a quarter million dollars annually in sales.

So this creative brainstorming section of the meeting became incredibly valuable for the team as a whole, as the company not only made more income, but the salespeople had an easier time selling more for the company as a result.

Successes

This part of the meeting was simple, but inspiring. The sales staff would get to share the successes they had in the past week with handing customers in situations that used to cause them trouble, applying tools they learned in earlier sales meetings, and even the fun they had selling the new products or using the new promotional materials. It was a time to share the good things about their week, and what the individual wins were.

Call it the 'heartwarming' part of meeting if you wish, but it was inspiring. They would share stories about happy customers, and we would read letters sent in by happy customers to the group. This was the part of the meeting where realization hit them that they were helping people, and bringing happiness and joy into their lives with our products and services.

The sharing of wins and successes became so infectious, that the sales people were inspired to try harder in the week to offer top customer service and friendship to customers they worked with just so that they had something special to share at the next meeting. This became so important a part of the meeting that whomever came to the meeting with the agreed upon best story of the week got a prize, which was usually something simple like a chocolate bar, $5 gift card, etc. It became a smaller game which became a rivalry, and winner was voted in my majority or decided by myself as the sales manager if it was too close to call. Sometimes I awarded two or more winners to continue to kindle the spirit of fun in the activity.

It was during this time at specific meetings that we awarded *salesperson of the week*, and every four weeks, *salesperson of the month* which I will discuss in more detail in later chapters. It was also a time when we would announce if a particular salesperson reached a 'highest personal best' sales week and we would applaud them too.

News and Updates

It was in this section of the meeting that we covered price changes, specials, packages, sales, etc. that the company was offering for the next week or month. We also announced plans for new products, promotions, etc. If a new product had been introduced that week, we went over it, and made sure everyone's questions were answered.

We also discussed any other logistical issues with the company from other areas, including changes in the paperwork or procedures to be applied with orders, etc. Other things covered were schedule changes, coming holiday schedules, and events going on the community that we needed to be aware of, as well as company promotional actions outside of the showroom that needed coordination, etc.

Throughout the week, I would note down issues that came up and needed to be addressed with the team. I was able to do away with memos, and stay organized by jotting down issues to address in this section of the meeting each week. I kept a clipboard in my office that even the salespeople could come in and write down information on throughout the week to be covered in this section, so I would not overlook something that was important to them. They could write down notes about needing pricing information or clarification on a new product, or service fee, etc. Essentially if it was not an urgent matter requiring immediate address, it was written down and covered at the upcoming meeting in this section.

Summary on Sales Meetings

So in summary, sales meetings were the most successful tool at my disposal as a sales manager. It made the entire team become cohesive and work together, and get to know and like each other.

It became a fun place to work, and a rivalry. New people benefited from the wisdom of other sales people, and became team members much faster. Older more seasoned sales people learned new ideas from the new people as well, and began to look after the new team members and help them when I was not around.

We all learned from each other, participated and made successes grow from failures each week. Soon the team became incredibly irresistible and persuasive as salespeople. So much so, that we lost so few sales to other competitors and the company grew into being the largest in the metro area of Atlanta. We gave no thought to the competition after awhile, and instead focused on *our own growth* and self improvement as individuals and *as a team*.

This same model can be used with any sales team, anywhere. Whether they can physically meet each week in a single location or not, you can always hold a meeting online and carry a similar format. Sales meeting are a time to unify a team, teach them new skills, share ideas and coordinate companywide strategies. This is a vital tool to a sales manager's success.

It becomes a refinement process over time of sharpening the skills of your team, keeping them unified, and focused on common objectives. Disjointed groups that meet infrequently cannot compete very long against a well organized team.

If you sincerely wish to maximize efficiency, and finally realize that previously out of reach level of running a unified team on all cylinders *at full throttle*; there is no better way than through educational, interactive and productive sales meetings which get results.

SECRET #11

Recording & Learning from the Past

The mind of an individual could be said to be ones brain and storage system of memories. The mind of any business is its records and files of the past. Because a business often involves many individuals, to recall its past it requires a system of records that is either in the material or digital storage universe.

As a small business sales manager, what records are going to be the most important to future sales? Certainly it is logical to consider most any financial record the business has to be useful. This goes without saying.

However, the records that most any sales manager really needs are typically the records that they do not keep. How can this be? What possible records could be more important than financial records?

Let's examine this. Suppose you as a manager held a sale on a particular weekend in June, and it was a great success. Would you not want to have a record of all the actions before, during and after the sale so that they can be repeated the following month or at least the next time June comes around?

How can you do this with simply financial records alone? The truth is you *cannot.*

In order to really learn from the past one must have a record of it as it happens. There are many ways a sales manager can do this, and here are few examples:

> ➢ Hand written log books
> ➢ Sales reports from salespeople
> ➢ Inventory Orders
> ➢ Photos of the set up for the sale
> ➢ Photos of the sale in action
> ➢ Surveys of customers
> ➢ Feedback from customers
> ➢ Digital logs and records

Have you ever watched an episode of the TV series 'Star Trek' and seen the Captain or another crew member open the show with *"Captains Log Star Date..."*? This may sound familiar, but it is an actual practice that comes from nautical navigation.

Any ship that has traveled the sea be it military or commercial has captain's logs, navigation logs, cargo manifests, etc. These records are kept so that others who come across them in the future can see what happened to the ship, learn from it and understand it. Even commercial airline flights have a 'black box' recording device capturing all information about every flight including pilot communications, navigation and other plane functions for every trip.

Consider these ideas as a sort of a *dairy of an explorer*. As a business owner, if you are trying new things, you are an explorer. Imagine yourself in the role of an explorer in the Amazon for a moment. Suppose you were to come to discover a long lost gold mine? Would you not want to have a record of how you got there? Keeping a diary of your journey, adventures and plans can help you re-trace your path to be able to return to a place you have been again in the future.

Record keeping for a sales manager trying to repeat the success of a prior event should include some of the key pieces of information:

- ➤ A record of the advertising done before the event
- ➤ A record of the sales from that date
- ➤ A record of what products sold and in what quantities
- ➤ The names of the sales team members working the day of the sale
- ➤ A count of the number of customers that came in
- ➤ A photo record of the display and set up for the event

> ➢ A photo record of the event as it happened
> ➢ Basic data on the time, date of the event
> ➢ A record of the weather conditions of the event
> ➢ A record of what was happening in the community that could have impacted the people in the area
> ➢ Feedback from customers who attended the sale
> ➢ Surveys of customers who attended and bought items at the sale
> ➢ Inventory records at the time of the sale
> ➢ Reports from the sales people who worked the event and experiences they had
> ➢ A log report written by the sales manager on any information that he/she deemed important to note about the occurrences at the event, and the any information of customer responses observed

Having a system in place that can capture the above information and place it in a file for future use would be invaluable for future efforts to re-create such an event.

In fact a sales manager should not just keep records of events and sales, but they should keep a running log of every day the business is open. That way when one comes to the end the month and really tries to examine what happened to the sales totals for the month, they have some records to investigate.

Keeping a computer record system in this day and age is quite easy. Here is the basic list of items you will need to put in such as system:

- A computer
- A printer/copier/scanner
- Word processing software (such as Microsoft Word, or some similar program)
- A basic understanding on how to use a computer, create files, and documents.
- A calendar

The system I am suggesting here is simple. The more you use it you can expand upon it or modify it to suit your needs.

Here are the steps:

- Take the calendar and create a file for each month or week (your choice) on your computer.

- Create some basic report forms with information you want to know to have your sales people fill out daily. It can include the hours they worked, number of customers they saw, items the sold, feedback they heard from customers, etc.

- Print out these basic report forms and give a stack to each sales person, and ask them to fill them out daily before leaving.

- Type out a report for your role as the sales manager, and note your observations on the day.
- Save all typed reports in the file for that day of the month or week, and place it in that folder on the computer.

- Scan all the handwritten reports turned in by the sales people, save those docs in the same file.

- Whenever an event is held, make more detailed reports covering information defined earlier in this chapter.

- Store all records of daily events in the file.

- Also store a roster of your sales staff at least once a month in the same files.

If you can do the above, you will have the beginnings of a record system you can refer back to and learn from. You can rediscover what actions you used to do that somehow fell out, and also discover actions that you should have done to improve things.

Records are a great way to learn from the past, and perform better in the future. One can get caught up in keeping to much information, and get overwhelmed and have the whole system become cumbersome as well. So it is best to start simple, and get in the pattern of recording basic data you need to remember. Hand written reports are easy to start with, and with a scanner they can all be saved as a PDF (Portable Document File) format.

If you do not want to use a computer, you can keep a written log book and paper file cabinets. However you decide to do this, the most important thing is to keep the records in such a way that you can find the information you need in the future without any difficulty.

Cloud Based Storage Systems

If you want to keep the entire record system in online in a cloud-based storage, here are a few examples to check into:

Dropbox.com – They have an easy system to store files online by dropping your documents right into a file on your desktop on your computer. Should your computer ever crash, your records are secure online.

Evernote.com – A multi-feature website where you can store information in the form of notes, photos, links, etc. all on a web-based format. You set up an account for free, and you can create files, documents, notes, etc. and organize it however you choose. You can also access this information anywhere on your computer, tablet or smart phone through handy apps.

Google Docs – Works through a Google email account. You can store docs and files online and organize them however you wish. You can also store photos, and other important information.

Summary on Records

Whatever system you set up, the most important thing to remember is that the records have to be accessible and the system has to work for you. If it is too complicated, you will have trouble with it and not use it. The best system is one that you can comfortably use and works for you.

SECRET #12

Counting, Tracking & Sharing Testimonials & Success

An error that many small businesses make is to overlook the importance of past client testimonials. The best promoters of any business are the happy customers who just purchased your products or services.

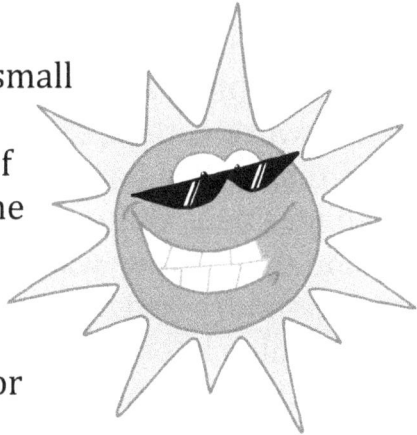

Certainly there is a magic that comes with positive 'word-of-mouth' promotion as former clients share their successes with other prospective clients and those prospects reach out for the same. However, it takes time waiting for these referrals to come naturally on their own. It also takes a volume of happy customers to see the impact of this, as not every customer will refer, even if they are satisfied.

The best way to give the magic of word of mouth advertising a boost is to have a system in place that captures client testimonials. There are many ways to do this, but the best timing is at the closing of the sale when they are wrapping up the paperwork. When asked, some people will jot down a few words right then for you, and others will ask to take it home and send it to you later. Either way is fine, however sometimes clients forget to mail it in.

Gathering client testimonials requires creative thinking at times. Here are a few more ideas and strategies that will help you with this:

Have a prepared testimonial sheet included in the paperwork with you wrap up the sale. Slide it in front of them when you are wrapping the sale up, and hand them a pen. Quite often they will fill it out right there and then. If they want more time, provide them with a pre-addressed envelope with postage on it to fill out and mail in later. If they do say they will mail it in later, have them fill out a reminder postcard with their own address on it and tell them you will keep it for a week and mail it to them if you have not received it.

In the process of the sale, be sure to collect the clients email address and mailing address. When you want future testimonials, you can mail or email them and ask for it. Offer them a coupon or a free giveaway like tickets to a show or local sporting event in return for a testimonial. This is an after the sale approach, and it works well.

Keep testimonial sheets in the showroom, and with all the salespeople. Ask them to liberally ask for client testimonials and feedback whether or not they make a purchase. Have them turn these in when they have them.

Instruct your receptionist who answers incoming calls to be alert for happy customers. If they speak to a customer who has good positive feedback, have them ask the client then and there if they would be willing to send them a testimonial in writing. Have the receptionist give out an email address for this purpose, or a fax line number. This can be a great way to collect this. Also if the client walks in, the receptionist is often the person they speak with and they should have testimonial forms to hand to give to a happy customer and ask them to write down a few words in person.

Add a web form on your company website where former clients can fill out testimonials there as well.

An important thing to include in all testimonial forms is a line at the bottom that the person signs and checks or initials a box that authorizes your company the right to publish what they write. These signed forms should be kept on file in case anyone was to come back and say they did not authorize the use of it.

Additionally, any email or web forms should also include some type of check box or passage that asks them to confirm what the person writes is okay to publish. Never publish one in marketing that is not authorized by the client.

Another safe practice is to not publish the client's full name on when using the testimonial in advertising, but instead just use their initials. You can also just publish their first name and an initial for their last name as well.

By having such a practice, you can tell the client you will use their initials only, and it might compel the ones who are hesitant to write one for you. If you want clarity on this, you can also include on the testimonial a check box if it is okay to use their full name or would they prefer initials only. That way there is no question.

The Use of Testimonials

Testimonials for happy customers should be included in all of your advertising. Print advertisement, brochures, websites, emails, newsletters, etc.

The sharing of the news of satisfied customers helps to build word of mouth. If you are mailing a newsletter to a list of former customers, and you include testimonials, it can spark other people to read and share it, especially if they had a similar experience. This is a great way to get former clients to refer business to you.

Also, by having testimonials on a website or other advertising, it helps the reader to see that there are other people using your products and services and they are happy about it.

We are in an age of online reviews about all kinds of businesses through websites like Yelp.com and many others. Encouraging your clients to post positive reviews there can also help with future business. A bright idea on this might also to have a computer set up in the showroom that gets people to write a review right there online while in the store. One can also have a place for them to write reviews on your company website through an online forum.

Summary on Testimonials & Success

The important point to take from all of this is that former customer reviews can help your future business. That is why it is also important to not only to constantly collect them, but also keep a count of how many you have on file too.

Boasting the number of positive testimonials one has for a company can also be another message to include in marketing. Businesses that collect, count and share positive feedback from former clients in their marketing fuel the fires of future sales.

SECRET #13

Building a Bright Idea Repository

Do you keep track of bright ideas? Do you encourage your sales staff and employees to develop bright ideas for the company and openly share them? As a small business sales manager one should consider setting up a bright idea repository with your company.

What is a bright idea repository? It is a system to collect bright ideas and preserve them. Sometimes a bright idea can be used right away. Sometimes they are not useful or applicable. Sometimes they are something that would make sense to implement in the future. Why not keep a record of such ideas?

The Suggestion Box

Many businesses have been built around the suggestion box. The suggestion box you see in some stores is essentially an idea box. Customers come to the store, and have an idea about an item or service they would like the store to provide and they write the information on a piece of paper and put it in the box.

Some may consider a suggestion box as old fashioned or 'old school', however it is nevertheless a potent and effective way of getting information that one would not likely get otherwise. Having suggestion boxes for customers and also for employees is a smart strategy to collect information one might not otherwise get. Also, as an unexpected benefit, a suggestion box can often reveal personnel situations and problems that might otherwise remain hidden.

A Bright Idea Repository

The concept of a 'bright idea repository' is essentially to establish three fundamental activities within the company:

- ➤ The freedom to create and share ideas on how to improve the company and its services
- ➤ The sorting, cataloguing and filing of these ideas for use now or in the future
- ➤ Use the best ones and make it known in the group who helped to create the idea.

As a small business owner or sales manager, one should encourage the sales staff and any other employee to share their ideas on how to improve the company.

The sharing of these ideas should be wide open and without liability for suggesting any idea, no matter how outlandish. They should be free to submit all of their ideas whether those ideas are good, bad or ugly.

Keep the Bright Ideas Flowing

The moment an idea is suppressed or thwarted, the entire flow of all future ideas gets choked. For example, let's say an employee who is always critical submits a suggestion to fire you as the sales manager or discard a project you worked so closely on and have personal feelings about. If you were to react and scold that employee, or embarrass them in front of others for submitting such an idea, or fire them, etc.

You would not only send a loud and clear message that not all ideas are welcome; you would make anyone who considers submitting an idea to second guess whether they should do so.

The moment you create an environment where the sales staff or employees feel they need to be careful with their suggestion of ideas, then all you will get are benign, 'careful' and boring ideas. The best way to address a critical 'idea' submission is to meet with the person privately and try to resolve the grievance.

So the best mindset is to be willing to experience any suggestion anyone might throw at you. Be willing to simply read it, and acknowledge and thank they person for submitting the idea. *No matter what it is!* Just thank them and let them know you received it. You do not have to commit to acting on it, or anything. All you have to do is let them know that you received it, and leave the door open for them to submit more ideas.

By behaving in this manner, you make it safe for them to be creative and after a time the real clever and useful ideas will start to roll in.

Organize the Bright Ideas

So the first step is to make it safe for anyone to submit their ideas and get those ideas flowing in. The next step is to organize and sort the ideas. Keep a filing system either in a physical filling cabinet or record the ideas in a series of computer files.

Organize them by date, subject and how practical they are for starters. You can create whatever cataloguing system you want. What is important is that you organize it in such a way that you can access it freely and make use of them when you can.

It is important also to acknowledge the person whose bright idea you implement in the company. Make sure they are publicly thanked within the group for their contribution (Unless for some reason they requested to remain anonymous). You might even give the person a bonus in pay if the idea is a real boost for the company.

Another point to address is that whenever you engage in idea collection that you make it clear to all employees that if an idea is implemented (such as a new product) that the company becomes the owner of this idea, as they created this while an employee of the company and were paid for doing so.

The easiest way to do this is to have all the employees sign a paper clearly stating that they understand that all copyright and patents from products created based on employee ideas submitted are the property of the company.

Summary of the Bright Idea Repository

Using this concept of a bright idea repository and collecting as many bright ideas as you can, will become an incredible resource over time. Sometimes an idea suggested in the present will require several months or years to implement.

However, having these ideas on file can help with future planning and the introduction of new products, services, etc. It may be the idea of today is really something that will be a huge success tomorrow. Keeping files and records of ideas, and then going back through them on a regular basis whenever the executives of a company are engaged in future planning sessions can be an exciting activity.

Sometimes just revisiting idea files that are old can trigger new ideas for the current planning. You never know when one idea may spark another. So keep the ideas coming in, organize them so they are not lost or forgotten, and thank everyone involved when one is executed. That is really the very basic if setting up and using such a system.

SECRET #14

Specials, Sales & Incentives

Every consumer loves a special. Everyone loves to get an item they are purchasing on sale. Whenever there is a customer incentive to make a purchase the pot is sweetened a little more.

Businesses develop and use all manner of specials, sales and customer incentives to fuel the purchasing mindset of customers.

In this chapter we are going to discuss three important concepts:

1. Sales
2. Specials
3. Incentives

At first glance one may assume there is no difference between these terms. All three could be considered to be terms used interchangeably with each other.

However, they are all distinctly different in their use for a small business sales manager. Each is a separate tool in the toolbox for boosting sales.

Sales

A sale is defined as: An event used for the rapid disposal of goods at a discount or with added value.

Holding a sale sticks in many people's mind as strictly being a discount for the purpose of clearance. However, a sales manager can host a sale for a variety of purposes. It is advertised to the public as a sale to draw them in, but there can be many reasons behind holding a sale. Here are a few common ones:

- ➤ Inventory clearance making way for new incoming inventory
- ➤ To boost sales during a seasonally slow month or quarter
- ➤ To sell off overstock of certain goods
- ➤ To capitalize on higher traffic periods to maximize inventory turnover

There can be many thinking processes behind using the sale as an event to draw in customers. As you can see, it is not just something that should be held when times are slow and one needs to increase business, but also during times that are busy to maximize cash flow for the business.

The set up for a sale typically incorporates special interior and exterior signage on the business to attract attention. It also includes specialized advertising both in print and online, as well as radio and television when appropriate to draw attention to the event.

Hosting a *sale* can be a great tool to boost income for a business in terms of goods sold. It can also become an over-used event if done too often. It is usually best to repeat successful sales annually (i.e. 'Year-end Inventory Clearance Sale') and if others are done, give them a unique characteristic to distinguish them from other sales. Here are some examples ideas of types of sales:

➢ Valentine's Day Sale
➢ Independence Day Sale
➢ Thanksgiving Sale
➢ Back to School Sale
➢ Internet Only Sale

Sales are a tool best used to give a boost to income. It can also be a refreshing tool for salespeople to use with certain clients they have been working on for awhile without successfully closing them.

It is also a reason to communicate with old customers, and send them mail and email notifications of the special event and opportunities, so they can tell others.

Specials

The 'special' is more of a specialized type of sale unique to an individual item or service. Businesses have been using the special for many years to draw in sales of other products and services. It typically surrounds the scenario of having one product in the inventory being offered at an extreme discount for a limited time.

Examples of the use of a special for a product would be something like the following:

> ➢ An auto dealer might place one style of mini-van or sports car at a low discounted price for the month of July and promote it broadly in all advertising and promotion. The vehicle may even be marked at a slight loss in profit to draw attention to the special.

> ➢ A restaurant might offer a particular menu item or dessert at a discount for the month or include a free item when a particular item on the menu is ordered during that month.

> ➢ An auto repair place offers a free set of wiper blades with every oil change during the month of August to build clientele.

> ➢ A lighting store offers 'two for the price of one' special on the sale of a certain brand of lighting for a specified time period.

Specials are a way for a small business to attract attention to the store or section of the inventory. Having an item on special in order for it to work must conform to two simple rules in order for it to work successfully:

1. It has to be an item or service people desire or want

2. It has to be an easily recognizable value in the discounted price offered for it to draw attention and interest

If it does not conform to the above two rules, it will not be successful. Offering an item on special that has been in the warehouse for months because it did appeal to buyers may work as a special if the item originally was priced to high and people were simply turned off by the price. However, if did not sell because *no one wanted it at any price*, then it will not work well as a special no matter how you try to present it.

One can also offer a special where the customer buys one item and receives a free gift or free service along with it. It works best if the free gift or service is a desirable item. Here are a few examples of how this can work:

➢ A company selling garage doors offers free installation for any purchase over $1000 in the month of April.

➤ A business that sells custom entry doors offers a free lockset with every purchase of a door in the month of September.

➤ A printer offers to double the amount of business cards printed when placing multiple orders.

➤ An online company offers free shipping for orders over $50 in December.

➤ A flower shop offers a free bouquet to anyone former customer who refers a friend and they place an order.

Using a special can take some imagination to make the idea unique and different to a prospective customer. The best way to approach this is to make sure that the idea comes across as interesting and fresh to the customer.

One great way to find the best type of special is to survey existing or former customers on what they would have liked to see as a special. Get their recommendations, and when you offer it make it available to them.

Incentives

Sales incentives could best be defined as: An offer of a service, discount or item of added value that motivates or encourages a prospective buyer to commit to a purchase.

Incentives are those tools used by a sales manager to help a salesperson close a deal that is stalled or on the edge of committing and the customer is just hesitant.

Incentives are best used in two specific formats as tools:

1. An incentive the salesperson has the authority to offer under certain conditions to make a sale happen.

2. An incentive the sales manager can offer at their discretion to help a salesperson finalize a sale.

Let's examine each of these individually and explore their potential use.

An incentive the salesperson has the authority to offer under certain conditions to make a sale happen.

This would be a pre-determined discount a salesperson is trained on and empowered to offer the customer under certain pre-defined conditions. These conditions are usually defined criteria such as the following:

> ➤ Only use this after you have offered the customer three other products to lower their price and meet their budget.

> ➤ Only use this incentive if the customer is determined to walk away and 'think about it'.

> ➤ Only use this item when you have written the entire job or sale up for the person and you have everything they need and want, and they still will not sign or commit.

There can be many guidelines established by a sales manager for his or her sales people that they must follow before they offer the incentive, or there could just be a simple few. It is really up to the sales manager and the way they choose to operate.

Incentives are best used as the last resort when all conventional methods to close the sale have been exhausted. Using an incentive precisely will make the use of it result in a sale. Using it incorrectly will result in no sale.

An incentive should only be offered with a strict condition. Here are some examples:

> ➤ *"Mrs. Jones, I can offer you a today only special discount on this purchase of 10% off if you agree to commit today..."*

> ➤ *"Mr. Edwards, I can throw in free delivery of your furniture if you place your order today. Sign here..."*

> ➤ *"Mrs. Johnson if you will agree to sign today, I can offer you a free installation of that new counter top and cabinet..."*

No matter the wording or the terms, the condition is: *We will offer you this great incentive, but you have to commit right now if we do.*

Omitting to require *action* from the customer in the offering of a special incentive is to invite the customer to not commit and wait to see if you will offer more. An incentive offered in this manner should result in a closed sale, not a continued negotiation.

An incentive the sales manager can offer at their discretion to help a salesperson finalize a sale.

An incentive offered by the sales manager works much the same way as it does if a salesperson uses it, but with two subtle differences:

1. It implies authority

2. It is clear to the customer this is the bottom line, final offer.

To bring in the sales manager to help one out with a customer who needs a push to commit is an effective way to operate with a sales team. It requires only two things from a salesperson to use this method as a means to salvage a sale:

A willingness to seek outside help from their sales manager

A willingness to stand back silently and let the sale manager take over the sale for a brief moment and close the customer

Salespeople that are trained well have no trouble asking for help. They know that the activity of sales is sometimes a team effort. Salespeople that learn to work with their sales manager in the use of this authority tool become masters at controlling the customer and the sales process. These are the keys to success.

It does not matter what incentive the sales manager offers. It could be of little or no tangible value to the company. What makes this approach effective is the delivery of the incentive to the customer from a position of authority who asks for a commitment from the customer in doing so.

Many companies build in room for a discount to be offered in this fashion. It is often expected. Not every customer asks for it, and not everyone receives this.

It is up to the company and the sales manager to decide what discount will be offered to whom and under what circumstances. However, one underlying rule must be used before an incentive is offered. It is that the customer agrees to commit, if a special incentive is offered.

Buyers who were never serious will be exposed for their lack of commitment during this process. Buyers who are serious will sometimes commit before every finding out what the discount or incentive is.

Summary on Sales, Specials & Incentives

The use of a sale is a powerful tool to draw in customers, new and old alike. Specials also help to boost sales from a difference time oriented perspective. Incentives have many uses, and can come in many varieties. All three are all vital tools for a sales team to have available and use at the right moment to increase sales.

SECRET #15

Effective Planning

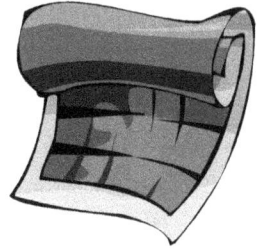

Planning is an important part of any business activity. Having a strategy in place of where one is striving to go is how a business owner and sales manager direct an operation. One could associate planning to a roadmap into the future.

A business plan is a clear defined set of goals that one lays out to obtain for the benefit of the company. It includes a description of the belief as to why those goals are considered to be obtainable, and a plan for reaching them.

There can be many plans within plans as one takes on such a task. If one has a 5 year business plan to reach a certain size for the company, as an example, then one would want begin breaking down yearly, quarterly and monthly plans one would need in order to make the overall plan a reality.

Plans & Execution

Plans that sit in a drawer without being acted upon ever achieve the reality of the dreamer who drafted them.

The one who draws up such company plan must be willing to not only share those plans with others, but also see to it that they are put on the road to being executed. Even if the one who drew up the plans is not the one who takes on the responsibility to put them into reality, the dreamer must at least hand those plans off to someone who will.

Plans require execution, or they do not work. So therefore we have a breakdown of various roles in such a subject of planning.

We have the one who dreams up the plan, the one who executes the plan and anyone else involved in the projects and tasks related to making the goals a reality as defined in the plans.

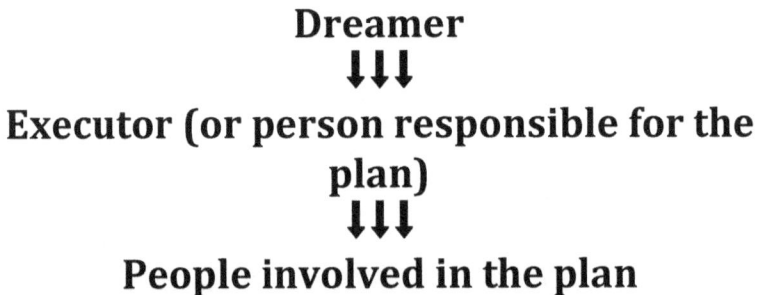

Dreamer
↓↓↓
Executor (or person responsible for the plan)
↓↓↓
People involved in the plan

Each has their part as one can see in the above example. One flows into the other down from the dreamer all the way to execution.

The dreamer of course can be the executor or responsible person, and he or she can also be the one entirely involved in achieving the goals. A company of one is set up in such a way. However, such a basic flow can translate to a larger group as well.

Types of Plans

Plans can break down into short term and long terms plans. It is best to think of them in the following terms:

1. Short range plans: 1 week to 1 month long maximum
2. Quarterly plans: Breaking down the year into four parts
    ➤ January – March
    ➤ April – June
    ➤ July – September
    ➤ October – December
3. Yearly plans: 12 months or calendar year plans
4. Long range plans: 2-5 years in length

A sales manager can assign and designate responsibility for planning to others in short increments when one thinks in the above terms. If one has assistants, one could take on planning the sales and events in each of the months in the existing quarter to align with quarterly goals for example.

Plans become more detailed the shorter they are, and more loose and flexible the longer they are. So one would likely set larger and broader goals on the long range plans, and then break each of these larger goals down in the yearly plans, and then quarterly plans until finally sections of each step are worked in detail as one executes the short range plans.

Keep the Planning Simple

Although the short range plans are often more detailed, they should never stray into the realm of becoming too complicated. Having a short term plan too complicated or overly detailed can result in the overall execution of it getting mired down.

Keeping planning simple is the most important thing to remember. Too much demanded in too short a time can result in important steps getting skipped, passed over or neglected. It is better to sort out what the most important things needed from each plan, and highlight those as primary targets, and identify the remainder in the plan as secondary targets, tertiary targets and so on.

Primary Targets = Most important results needed to be met to keep the overall planning on track.

Secondary Targets = Important steps, but the overall plan will not be compromised if they are not successfully completed in the timeframe defined.

Tertiary Targets = Steps that would be nice to have done, but are not vital or have little or no impact to the plans overall success.

Keeping planning simple means: *identifying the primary targets, and working on those first before allowing time for the other ones.* In the execution of any plan it is easy to go off track from the overall goal by getting caught up into too many details.

Therefore, it is essential to be able to not only draw up an effective short range plan, but also being able to take that second step of going back through what one has strategized and classify the primary, secondary and tertiary targets. To be able to do this require just doing it and practicing it on small projects at first, and then expanding it out to more detailed ones later on.

Online Resources

There is a great mentoring organization that just turned 50 years old called **Score**. They offer a website with free resources for small businesses to help with subjects such business planning, financial forecasting, sales planning, marketing planning, etc.

Their website is: *www.score.org*

I highly recommend connecting up with then for ideas and help, as they have an advisory board of retired businesspeople that enjoy helping the small business owner and managers.

Another great resource is: *www.entrepreneur.com*

This is a company devoted to helping the small business entrepreneur, and their website is loaded with great ideas for business planning.

Finally, the small business administration has some nice resources of papers written on the subject of business planning on their website: *www.sba.gov*

Summary of Plans & Planning

It is advisable to compare a variety of business plan models before deciding on the best one for you. Get copies from different resources, and keep in mind the basic timeframes and targets discussed in this chapter and you will go far.

Always remember that keeping it simple means it is more likely to get done as opposed to having the plans become too complicated. If you can keep that in mind, you will experience great success in accomplishing your goals.

SECRET #16

Celebrating the Moments

Have you ever experience jubilation over a success in life? Salespeople who face a challenging job often have their highs and lows in the course of a day's work. Celebrations sometimes can come between long gaps of arduous work.

Have you ever witnessed in sports a player who just scored some points celebrating? In football it is the end-zone celebration dance. In baseball when a homerun it hit, it is the celebration of all ones teammates greeting them as they cross home plate.

In soccer it is that dynamic moment when a teammate scores a goal where the stadium erupts with excitement in the stands and also on the field. Every sport has its celebration. Every profession has them too.

I once heard the story of a diamond seller who used to celebrate his victories in sales with his own unique 'antler dance'.

It was a self-created dance where he leaned forward and placed the backs of his hands on his head with his fingers sticking out mimicking deer antlers, and he would prance around in a circle.

He only did this when he made such a big sale that he could not contain his excitement. To anyone witnessing it, they were either stunned or just smiled and laughed. It was his moment of joy and celebration that was uniquely his own.

Life is filled with challenges, and sometimes the road can be long and difficult. Taking the time to celebrate those moments of success is an important part of it. It is a release of tension, and the pure joy and fulfillment of a job well done.

Did you ever experience that freedom as a child where you could dance and it did not matter whether you knew anyone was watching or not? Somewhere as an adult, many of us lost that.

Perhaps is it the growing years where peer criticism and ridicule made one withdraw from doing such things for fear of embarrassment. It is different for many people, but some have a more difficult time with open celebration than others as an adult.

"You've got to Dance like no one is watching. Love like you'll never be hurt, Sing like no one is listening, and Live like it's heaven on Earth"
                                    - William Purkey

In those moments, just let loose and dance like no one is watching. You deserve it. The people that work with and for you deserve it to. Let them dance and celebrate. This is the best part of living.

Don't Neglect the Importance of Celebration

Too often a sales manager or small business owner fails to celebrate a success in an organization. They can get caught up in the wheels of production, and say 'Let's move onto the next project' and overlook the need to celebrate the recent accomplishments that so many on their team worked hard on. This can be a detriment to the morale of the organization if it happens too often.

One does not need to wait for a holiday to celebrate, nor does the cost need to be lavish or expensive. Sometimes it is just the recognition that the members of the team need, before moving onto a new goal on the frontier.

It could be "We have all worked so hard on this project, and now it is finished! How about we take the rest of the afternoon off?" Or it could be "Great job everyone on the monthly sales goal! Let's meet in the conference room for some take-out food on me." Whatever approach you decide to use or create, what is important here is that you let your people take a breather and enjoy themselves. If you do they will work harder on the next goal.

A sales manager can and should arrange for an occasional party for the sales staff to release tension, and highlight a recent group milestone or victory. If there is no milestone or recent victory, you can always celebrate an anniversary of some special date, and toast to the tenacity of the team.

Celebration as a Tradition

I have even witnessed a sales manager install a ship's bell in the conference room and ring it every time someone made a sale. You can also use a gong, or similar noise making device that makes a loud resounding noise.

The idea was not so much the ringing of the bell that salespeople looked forward to, it was when the bell was rung in their honor. That is what they strived for. Everyone attending sales meetings or even impromptu meetings during the course of a business day looked forward to that bell being rung because of what they accomplished.

Things like the bell or gong ringing in one's honor become a tradition, and the sales staff will begin to look forward to it and expect it. These kinds of things will also help to create good heart-warming memories about their experiences with the company, and make them more of a team member.

Another tradition I have seen used successfully is to have a notice board in the staff area where everyone can see and read. Post notices on how awesome certain team members are at various times, and draw attention to their successes. Show positive progress on company goals, and do not allow any negative items or messages to be posted on such a board. Share client success stories, and post pictures of happy satisfied clients receiving their products sold by the team, and acknowledge the salesperson who sold it to them.

Saying 'Thank You'

Hosting celebrations and creating an environment where salespeople feel it is safe to have fun at their jobs and celebrate success is the ideal stress free environment. As a sales manager or small business owner, taking time to say *'Thank You'* to your team for their hard work and dedication will inspire them to work harder for you. Failing to recognize them or simply thank them occasionally will quite often build up resentment and animosity.

Sometimes the best way to say 'Thank you' is to take the entire group out of the office they work so hard in all the time. Buy the whole staff tickets to the movies and make it an impromptu office trip to a matinee show. Or take them all out for some putt-putt golf, or give them all gift cards and take them all shopping at a popular store. Whatever it is, get them out of the environment for a while and have some fun.

Any business owner who has a sales department that has a sour attitude, or there exists a general bitterness or losing mentality can often be traced back to lack of acknowledgement for previous hard work. Managers and owners that remember to celebrate and say 'Thank you' to their team have the easiest job. A sales team that feels that the management cares about them, understands what they deal with, and recognizes their hard work will work harder. This makes a sales managers job a breeze.

Joining in the Celebration

The sales manager or small business owner can sometimes forget to celebrate themselves when an achievement or milestone has been reached. Taking time to celebrate with your sales staff is essential, and it gives you a chance to share in their joy too.

Joining the celebrations you hold for them means that you are not distancing yourself from them. You are connecting with them, and the understanding and respect will grow. If they see you distant and avoiding celebrations you arrange for them, they will see that too and it will work against you. Therefore the sales manager must also join in the celebration.

As a sales manager, it is also important to give yourself a break now and then too. Take an early night off, go to the gym or just spend time with your family. Celebrating has to be universal for both the leader and the ones who follow. So don't get caught up in the complexities of your next move or goal when it is time to celebrate a success.

Relax and put your planning aside for 24 hours, and just enjoy some rest, fun and laughter with those that you work so closely with. Get out there and enjoy life! If you can do this, you will achieve a balance which not every manager ever reaches.

Acknowledging Success Creates Success

When a sales manager acknowledges successes achieved by a group, it inspires future success. This comes about for several reasons:

It increases motivation – Not just in the group to repeat the success, but in you as a sales manager to challenge you to perform better.

It increases confidence – The team will become confident that they can rise to any challenge.

The overcoming of obstacles becomes easier – The group will be able to rally back from setbacks that can happen in sales, and lose very little time in doing it because they will believe in themselves.

It makes people happy – Putting a smile on the face of someone for a job well done makes them feel better.

When a sales team can feel free to let go and celebrate, cheer and just enjoy the game of the profession they are in, success continues to build upon success. After a time, it becomes easier and easier for all involved.

Never overlook the importance of celebration! It is the energy that keeps the world in motion.

SECRET #17
Admiration & Accomplishment

The underlying sparks behind the ambition of many people, whether they are aware of it or not, is the desire for *admiration*. What is admiration?

The definition of Admiration breaks down into two parts:

1) *A feeling of wonder, pleasure and warm approval from another.*
2) *To be the object of wonder and esteem; a marvel.*

So it is the flow coming from another in definition number one, and it is being the object of the flow from another in definition number two.

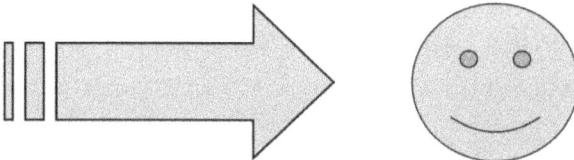

Understanding the importance of admiration when it comes to salespeople is important. Sometimes it is all that drives them to achieve greatness. As a sales manager, one must not only offer praise for accomplishing a task with great success. One should also remember to grant that person some personal *admiration* and see to it that they are held up to praise in the group, whereby they will also get *admiration* from the team.

Being admired for our accomplishments in life could be said to go back to childhood. A child is always seeking admiration from his or her parents for their accomplishments in life.

Parents who offer admiration freely will have a child who continues to thrive, and seek to accomplish more. When a child is cut off from admiration from their parents, the severing of this line can be painful and more destructive than many people realize. It could even be said to be the root cause of delinquency.

Working with groups of sales people, the principles are the same. People will work to achieve quotas and bonuses and even play games.

However, despite all the tangible rewards of a job well done, the most valuable sense of satisfaction one receives is when they receive admiration for doing so from others, especially those they consider important in their lives.

If you want to have a team that work together and individually to achieve your goals, then remember to sprinkle some admiration around from time to time and make sure it is genuine. Artificial admiration never works. It comes across as being insincere, and the result will become the opposite of what you desire.

A Simple Admiration Drill

If you want to practice the skill of giving admiration to your staff, then do the following simple drill:

1) *Go to a public place and look at people.*
2) *Select a person in the crowd, and find something about them that you can admire.*
3) *Once you have determined that you admire it, approach them and tell them so sincerely.*
4) *See how they respond.*
5) *Repeat 1-4 above.*

The more you do this, the easier it will become and the better you will understand the impact it has on others. You will also be able to achieve better control of that 'flow' of *admiration* discussed in definition number one above.

Admiration & Accomplishment

In the context of a sales manager and the application of admiration it is best understood when one is addressing a sales person in front of others. Perhaps in the context of a sales meeting a sales manager might call to the attention of the group an accomplishment of one of the members of the team.

In doing so, the sales manager should make is know how wonderful the accomplishment was, and make it clear that there is cause for admiration at the success of the individual. Whether expressed directly in words or not, the admiration for the accomplishment should come across clearly.

When one does this, there are two immediate outcomes from spreading around admiration:

1) The sale person who is the object of the admiration will feel the warmth of approval and satisfaction from the experience, and will seek to repeat or improve upon their prior success.

2) Others witnessing the admiration vicariously will seek to perform better at their own jobs in hopes of being the recipient of such admiration themselves in the future.

With this one can see that admiration could be called a particular wave of energy which has value to others. It is a simple, yet powerful bonding agent for any group in its drive towards a goal and achieving success. A business owner or sales manager who understands this energy will be able to harness it for the betterment of the group, and raise others up to new heights of accomplishment.

Summary on Admiration

Admiration is a powerful and valuable asset to the tools of a sales manager, and should be considered among the most important at his or her fingertips. One never knows when a simple flow of admiration to a sales team member on any subject will boost them up from at a time when they are struggling.

Everyone likes to be admired from time to time. Spread some around and watch the results as magic.

SECRET #18

Games & Rewards

One of the important lessons one can learn in the course of managing sales people is that one must include them in a game that they will play for. Games are a part of the fabric of life. To conduct a game with a sales team, it does not have to be complicated or expensive to administer. In fact you will find the simpler the game, rules and playing field; the easier it is for everyone to play.

Some of the best games are the status games that offer simple rewards, but bring proper admiration and acknowledgement of accomplishment to the winner.

Salesperson of the Week, Month & Year

One of the most successful sales games one can hold is the basic *'Salesperson of the week'*, *'Salesperson of the Month'* and *'Salesperson of the Year'* which can be implemented with most any company sales team. It consists of simple rewards, but it gives status among the members of a small group. It also can create a competitive rivalry between team members, which can be both healthy and fun for the morale of the group.

The *Salesperson of the Week* for the prior week is usually awarded at a weekly staff meeting. The winner can simply receive a printed paper certificate, and group recognition each week. At the sales meeting, make sure to announce who is front in the race for salesperson of the month and year.

For the *Salesperson of the Month* award, it most often is awarded to the highest earner of gross sales on the calendar month, but this can vary from company to company. The winner could their name engraved on a special company plaque or other display, which clearly states who was 'Salesperson of the Month for (year)' on the top along with the company name, and space below for 12 individual plates.

Plaques from a trophy shop are inexpensive and updating the monthly plates is also low cost. This is an affordable game to execute and the fact that the monthly winners name is engraved on a plaque is a proven and successful way to create competition. The winner also could receive a certificate at the sales meeting with a small gift or perk for the coming month like a special parking spot, or an extra day off, etc. Use your imagination and also survey what your team is interested in playing for.

The 'Salesperson of the Year' award should be much more special. An individual plaque or trophy should be made for the winner, and keep it consistent from year to year. The award recipient should be kept secret as much as possible during the last month of the year, and the December Salesperson of the Month is recommended to be awarded at the same ceremony only along with the 'Salesperson of the Year'. The best way to do this is to hold an awards dinner and have all the Salespeople invited with their spouses, at a nice restaurant or event facility. You can even arrange for a private room.

This should be your top annual award, and so make it important for all the Sales Staff. You can also award other smaller awards at the ceremony such as 'Come back sales person of the year' and 'Rookie of the year' for larger sales teams. Be as creative as you want on this. It is a low cost expense to purchase a few awards and recognize the annual performance of the people you so depend on. It can also be a great boost for their morale, and encourage them to perform higher the next year.

What you will most enjoy about this game as a sales manager is that it is simple and low cost to administer, yet it acknowledges the highest producers and gives them status. As a Sales Manager, one just has to keep tallies of the total sales of all the sales team, which you most likely do every week anyway. All of this information can be stored on a spread sheet and accounting software and totals are thus easy to keep track of. There are basic programs one can use such as Excel in Microsoft Office for example which can help you with this quite easily.

Other ways one can improve status, and reward those who excel are to give them an upgrade to their office, perhaps a new desk, or as mentioned before a parking space or other perk. Any of these can be incorporated into a status and reward program, and they create an environment of productivity if done correctly. Never play favorites because of personality, friendship or 'who is popular'. Always look at the individual's production, and reward them accordingly. Impartiality is what makes this a successful program, and gives all players an even playing field to perform at their best in a competitive environment.

Highest-Ever Acknowledgements

Another smaller award system that can be implemented is to call attention to a salesperson in front of the group at a meeting whenever they have hit a personal highest-ever in sales, no matter how it compares to everyone else. Make a point to acknowledging them at a next meeting in front of the group.

You might also prepare a certificate, or something like a card to give them. The most important aspect of this is the status it gives them among their peers, even if just for a moment. The longer they are with the team, the more significant their 'highest-ever' or 'highest personal best' acknowledgments becomes. The result will be that it challenges to do it again the following week as well.

In this way one can encourage a team to push themselves for higher production each week. Sometimes one can offer a cash bonus for 'Highest-Ever' for individuals in a given week, announcing it in advance and encouraging all of them to reach their personal best that next week. Some companies do this with their sales teams as a regular game. It works well to keep salespeople striving for higher targets each week. The *Highest-Ever* recognition can also be played as a group game, or combined with an individual game as well. It all depends on the creativity of the sales manager and how they want to execute such a game with their team.

Group Awards

Another game strategy that works well for groups is to offer a group goal to strive for week after week.

Here is an example:

Once I had purchased a company with some partners that was earning about $250,000 a year. My partners and I wanted to double that in our first year of new ownership. So dividing an annual goal of $500,000 total gross income across 52 weeks, the figure becomes about $9615.38.

Our solution was to round off the target up to an even $10,000 weekly and we launched the '10K' game. It was simple and everyone company-wide played hard to deliver as many orders and the few sales staff we had at the time would push hard for sales. So the company would make money from both ends, as with most of our orders we received payments of 50% down from customers and 50% on delivery.

The game ran from Thursday at 6:00 pm to the following Thursday at 6:00 pm. The award was that we would order pizza's for everyone to eat for lunch that Friday if we made it. It took a several weeks of close calls, and high production for the little company in that first year, but we soon hit the target and the pizza was perhaps the most delicious we as a group ever ate, simply because it was *hard won by all*.

In weeks that followed we continued to hit the target each week, and we were having pizza it seemed all the time, and the game itself became mundane. It soon became *too easy*. However, the company was now pacing 2X income from the year before. So we increased the goal and continued the game weekly.

The lessons one can learn from this regarding group goals is that jumping on a unique idea for a target not yet achieved for a group is an excellent way for them to come together and produce more together. Winning the 10K game in the above example gave the group sense of accomplishment, and everyone felt they contributed. The awards were simple, and one would be amazed how hard people will play for a *simple reward* like a pizza and an acknowledgment of a job well done. It does not have to be an expensive bonus, or a complicated game. Simple awards, with simple rules are all a group needs sometimes to come together to play a game.

Another way to structure such a game is to offer a weekly award such as a simple trophy that can be traded off each week to the new winner. Award the trophy at a staff meeting, and they earn the rights to keep it on their desk throughout the upcoming week. It is a simple sales game that can be successful for a group. The trick is to get everyone playing for it. If you can do this it can be a lot of fun.

Sales Games Bring People Together

Sales games bring a team of sales people together in a competitive environment. The game does not have to be complicated. In fact, from my experiences, whenever the game was complicated with too many rules, *no one played.* Awards were sometimes given in those circumstances, but it was more by chance that you won it than that you actually played for it.

One will be amazed with results from surveying a sales staff in an effort to discover what awards or games they will play for. As a sales manager, you might conclude they will only play for 'cash bonuses', and 'cash awards'. The truth is whenever I surveyed, I was surprised to learn that less than 10% even mentioned any kind of monetary reward. Do you know what I discovered the biggest item they wanted in the survey if they won? *An extra day off the week that they won!* They did not even ask to be paid, they just wanted the day!

The number two item on the survey was they wanted the sales manager to take them to lunch and pay for it. Again, not what I was expecting when I first did this survey. I was literally shocked looking up and down the survey results for mentioned of monetary rewards and found very few. The awards they would play a game for was not money, but simple things that were important to them like more free time and personal time to share ideas with the boss.

So the lesson one can learn from this is that one should survey and seek to discover what your team will play for. Do not let your own expectations or ideas determine this. Ask them to give it to you, and you may be surprised at the results you find.

Key points you will discover about sales people and surveys:

➢ Most sales people like to play games.

➢ As a sales manager, one needs to do surveys with the members of your sales team to find the *right* award that *they* will play for. Do not make the questions in the survey leading, or multiple choice, let them originate what they want. The results will surprise you.

➢ Never assume you know what they want, because 99% of the time you do not.

➢ Awards do not have to be simple or complex, but they can be fun.

➢ Status and recognition among their peers is often more important than monetary rewards.

Willingness

Obtaining a group or salesperson's willingness to play a game is essential in measuring the potential of any proposed game. If they are not interested, they will not play.

I was once in a sales position selling books for a small independent publisher, and I had to deal with a remote sales manager who thought she should call me daily, and check on my sales.

She would enforce games on me, and insist that I play these games of her own invention. I was in a smaller market, yet she expected me as a salesperson in a small market to compete with other representatives in larger markets like New York and Washington D.C.

Despite her continuous efforts to impose games on me, and her insistence that I play them, *I was not interested.* The game was not *my game*, nor was I surveyed. If I had ever been surveyed, I would have demanded an even playing field in the sales area. Also as my reward I would have asked that she only call *once a week*, rather that needle me on a daily basis.

After a number of years, I eventually left the job in frustration. However, after a number of years away, I can now look back on this and share this wisdom: *You must have the salesperson's willingness to play a game,* and *it must be a game they are willing to play.*

If you do not have these two things, you cannot very well succeed. You better do the following:

A) Find out *what* they would play for.
B) Find out *what game* they are *willing* to play.
C) Give them *that game*, and no other.

Ultimately if you do not, you will have no success in trying to impose a game. You will likely make the error of trying to discipline them, or foolishly enforce punishment, and then they will *never ever* play *any* game.

This of course eventually happened to me in that job, and I left, even though statistically I had made

more sales in that position than any of
my predecessors. The loss to the organization of my
production was brought about by a sales manager who
was not willing to listen, much less understand.

So as one can see from this example, in order to
get *willingness* from your team, as a sales manager you
must first be willing yourself to: *listen,*
survey and *understand*.

If you can do this, then you are then in a position
to suggest a game that the proposed players would be
willing to play. Then you will have accomplished the
most important thing in running a successful game
with them: *willingness to play*.

Summary on Games & Rewards

Games and rewards systems can be a vital and
important behind the scenes strategy to keep a group
working week after week for higher and higher
production. If you do not have some sort of game or
rewards system in place, and encourage people to
participate, you are going to struggle through tough
times. Games make for a competitive environment, and
this is a healthy way to keep a group alive and enjoying
their jobs.

Sales forces without games or rewards systems
in place are lifeless and unhappy environments to be in.
Boredom is a killer of income for a company. Keeping a
fresh outlook week after week takes work, and games

and rewards are the best way to do this. No matter what system you choose, just choose one that people are willing to play and that works for your company and you will succeed.

SECRET #19

The Magical Healing Power of Laughter

Far too often one can slide into a mental state where life is too serious. Seriousness after a time removes all the smiles from ones surroundings. If one can raise their own head for a moment above this seriousness, and consider something *unserious* for a moment, they just might *laugh*.

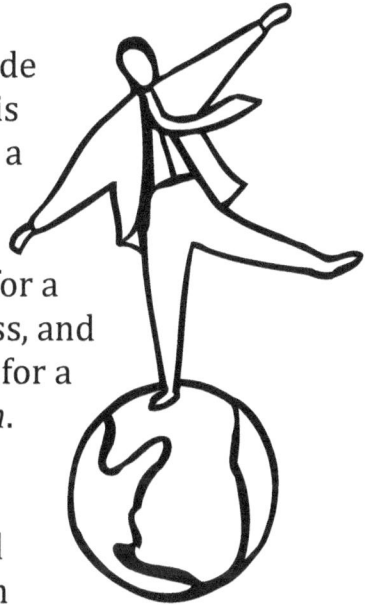

Laughter has long been regarded as powerful spiritual healing power. Much has been written about this throughout history. An ancient biblical proverb once claimed "*A merry heart doeth good like medicine*" asserting the power of laughter as healing properties.

Medical studies have shown that laughter can also strengthen the immune system, boost your energy and reduce physical pain. There is no greater stress reliever than a good rolling laugh. Laughter is a simple and easy way to reduce stress, pain and conflict in the environment as well.

Soldiers who serve together in war often share stories of laughter and fun with their brothers in arms more readily than their experiences on the battlefield. Laughter is more easily remembered because it brings joy.

In ancient times the court jester was brought in to ease tensions and relieve melancholy and bring merriment to royalty. Native American tribes like the Hopi and Cree had clown characters in their traditional ceremonies whose job was to provoke laughter and bring about lightheartedness.

Laughter is infectious. The sound of others roaring in laughter is far more contagious than any symptom of influenza. When one has a good hearty shared laugh with another, it binds them together in a way that did not exist before. To be able to laugh uncontrollably in uproarious laughter with a colleague, family member or friend will increase general overall happiness.

When one laughs together with family it fosters open communication, understanding and harmony. There is no more unmistakably powerful undercurrent to bringing people together than a genuine good laugh with those one loves.

The power of mirth can extend to any group and bring about a healthy relationship and serve as a binding agent that is hard to separate. In business and in sales there is no better way to build a team than to include some good hearty laughter and merriment in the course of daily operations.

Whenever a sales manager runs into a difficult situation with a sales person, one should always remember to fall back on the magical healing power of laughter. If one can sincerely laugh, he or she can get others to laugh as well, because it is infectious.

If you think about the last really good laugh you had for a moment, how did you feel? It probably made you feel good, didn't it?

Laughter is safer and far more effective to a person's well being than any pill produced by Big Pharma. There is nothing quite like a jiggling good ol' belly laugh with your eyes watering to really make your day feel lighter.

The sales manager who understands that the business of sales is a people business will be able to see that there is nothing more valuable to lighten tense situations than laughter. Mark Twain once wrote: *"Humor is mankind's greatest blessing"* and he could not have been more right.

The Test of Laughter

Getting another to laugh as a sales manager does not require that one have a book of jokes handy or a witty sense of humor. These kinds of things might be helpful, but they are not necessary. The best tool one can use is to simply ask someone to laugh.

As you read this I can see that you might be raising an eyebrow. Consider the following test with a group of people you might be speaking to:

1) *Ask the group to laugh*

2) *If they look at you with a blank stare, simply smile and ask them again to laugh and wait for them to do so.*

3) *Someone will laugh as a matter of course. It usually will be a mild hesitant laugh at first. No worries. Smile at them again and ask them to laugh some more.*

4) *Keep doing this until they are all laughing. Ask them to laugh, and then laugh some more. Do it over and over until they are all roaring a laughing. It works, just try it.*

They might laugh because they think you are crazy. That is fine. The test will reveal how infectious laughter is. It is possible to get the group laughing by just asking them over and over again to do so until the infectious nature of it kicks in and takes over.

The release of mirth will lighten the room and any troubles anyone was carrying on their shoulders will drift away.

Summary on the Magic of Laughter

Laughter has long been known to offer healing properties to the soul. It can ease tensions and stress, and lift a burdened spirit with joy. Using laughter to bring a group together and heal, as well as move on past a difficult time is the magical power of laughter. Use it.

FINAL THOUGHTS

The challenge for the small business in today's society does not lie in overcoming of the economic obstacles that seem to be ever growing. It does not lie in the climate, changes in politics or fashion. These things might have an impact on the short term, but they can be adapted for.

No, the true challenge for the small business manager today exists with the understanding and care for the people in society. Our business world revolves around people and interacting with them, and being skilled enough to control and direct them in such a way to sell them your products and services and bring about prosperity and survival for your team.

Without understanding fully the people equation, a sales manager is lost. This book was a journey and discovery of many tricks and tools for making business a success, but it also included gemstones to better relationships with people.

The chapters on knowing your customer, capturing their attention and the use of admiration and laughter to guide your way are just a few of the treasures we discussed. Planning for the future of your business, hosting events and staying connected with your customers will strengthen your survival as an organization.

Most important of all is understand the mentality of winning, and keeping strong with that vision in all the goals you pursue. That secret above all others is perhaps the greatest one of them all, and it is why it was offered as the first chapter in this book.

Take what you will from the pages of this book, and apply it to fuel the fires of prosperity for your business. In doing so, you will overcome all economic challenges and barriers that seek to present themselves as obstacles in your way. With a winning mentality, and an arsenal of secret weapons, nothing can stop you.

Cheers!

ABOUT THE AUTHOR

Michael Delaware is a Phoenix, Arizona native who now resides in Battle Creek, Michigan with his wife Margarita. He also lived in Georgia for 15 years in the 1980's and 1990's where he owned and operated a stained and beveled glass studio in the Metro-Atlanta area. During those years he was an active volunteer in the community, coordinating annual Arts and Crafts Festivals in the downtown district of Roswell, Georgia. He also participated in Arts & Crafts Shows for over 25 years as a vendor in numerous States. He has been a Michigan resident since 1999.

His other published works include numerous non-fiction books on real estate, sales management, marketing and other self-help topics. He has also published fiction and non-fiction stories for children.

As an illustrator and photographer, he has included his works in his own books and blogs. He enjoys hiking and mountain biking in the great outdoors and taking long walks in the woods with his dog.

Currently he is an active Realtor in Michigan and frequent community volunteer. He is a member of the National Association of Realtors, The Council of Residential Specialists, and the Michigan Association of Realtors. He is also an active member of the Battle Creek Area Association of Realtors where he was awarded 'Realtor of the Year' in 2010, and served as Board President in 2011. He founded his own independent publishing company in 2012.

To follow Michael:

www.MichaelDelaware.com

Facebook.com/MichaelDelawareAuthor

Amazon.com/Author/MichaelDelaware

Linkedin.com/in/MichaelDelaware

@MichaelDelaware

Other titles by the author:

(Available in paperback and eBook format unless otherwise noted)

The Art of Sales Management: Lessons Learned on the Fly

The Art of Sales Management: Revelations of a Goal Maker

The Art of Sales Management: 75 Training Drills to Build Confidence, Excellence & Teamwork

Small Business Marketing: An Insider's Collection of Secrets

Arts & Craft Shows: The Top 10 Mistakes Artist Vendors Make... *And How to Avoid Them!*

Arts & Craft Shows: 12 Secrets Every Artist Vendor Should Know

Inspiration: The Journey of a Lifetime *(eBook only)*

For Real Estate:

Understanding Land Contract Homes: In Pursuit of the American Dream

Land Contract Homes for Investors

Land Contract Homes: The Top 10 Mistakes Home Buyers Make... *And How to Avoid Them!*

Going Home... Renting to Home Ownership in 10 Easy Steps

In Children's Fiction:

Scary Elephant Meets the Closet Monster *(eBook only)*

In Children's Non-Fiction:

My Name is Blue: The Story of a Rescue Dog *(eBook only)*

For a current list of available print books visit:

www.ifandorbutpublishing.com

or

Amazon.com/Author/MichaelDelaware

If you found this sales management book useful, you might also like these other titles by the same author:

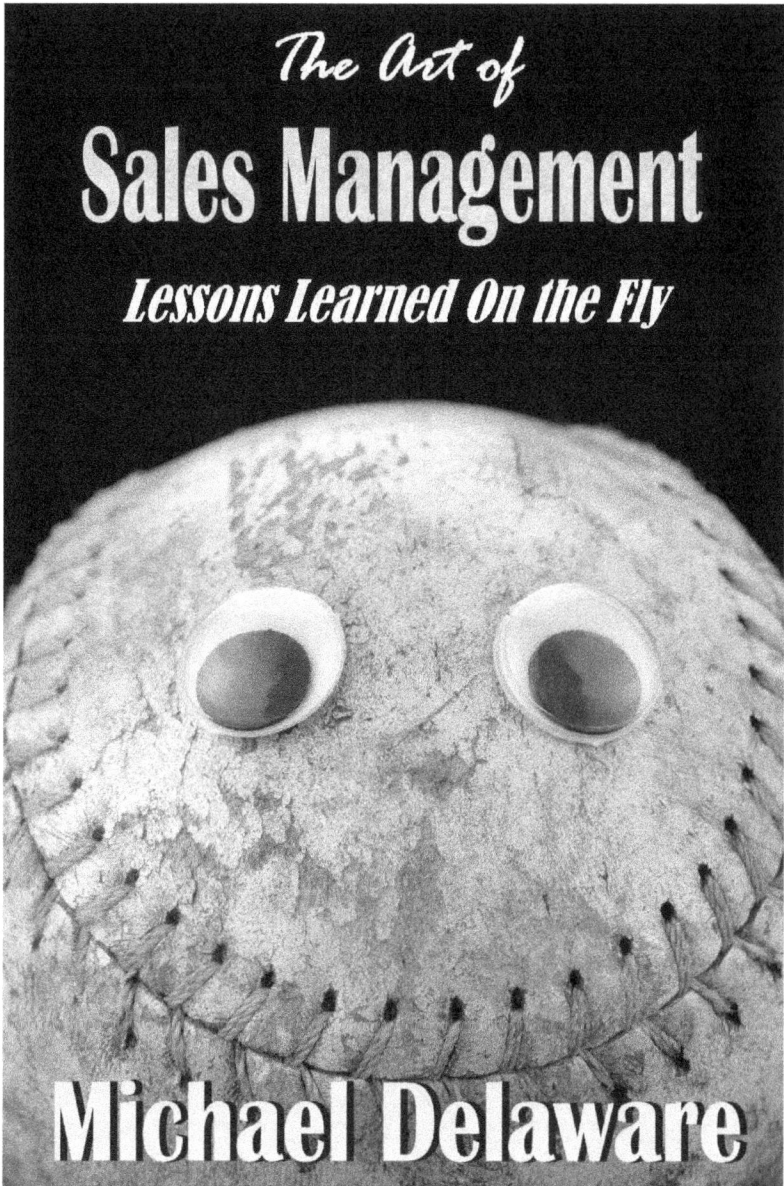

The Art of
Sales Management
Lessons Learned On the Fly

Michael Delaware

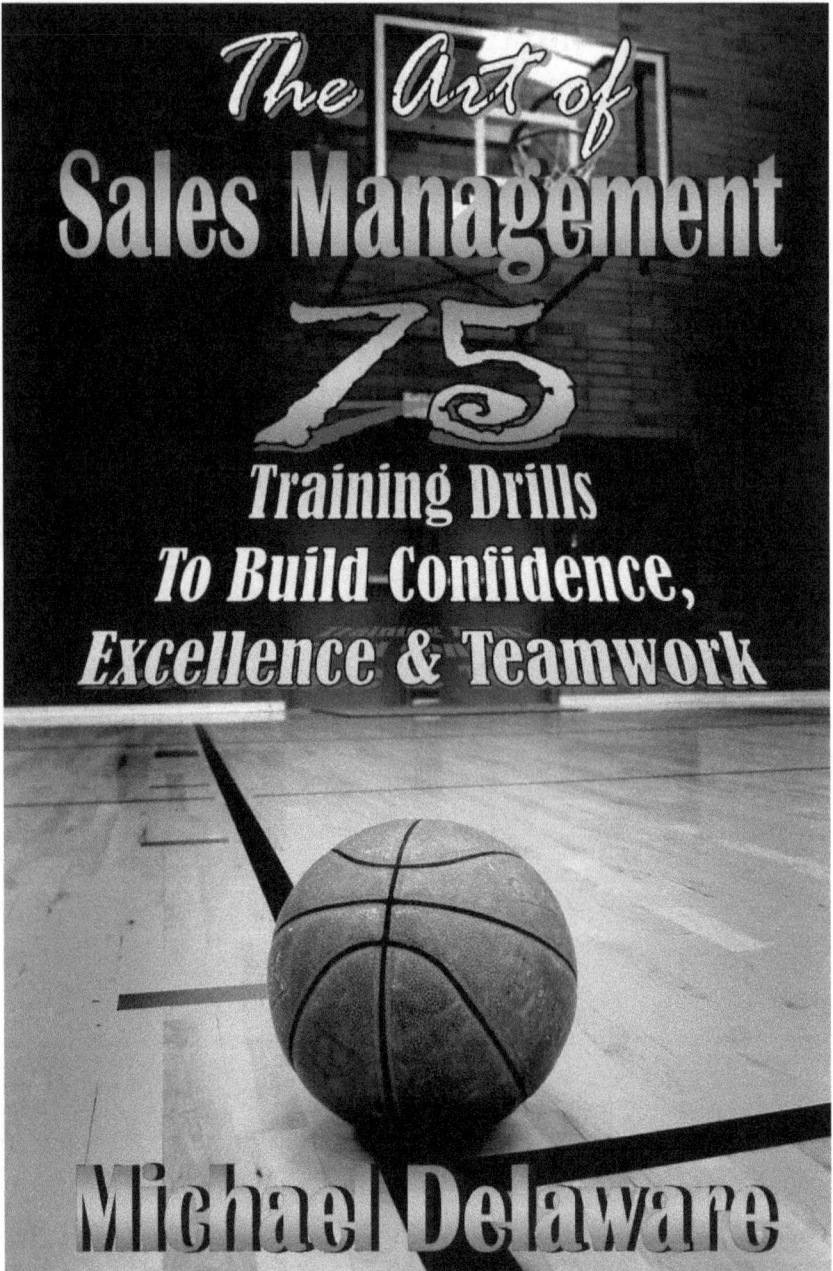

The Art of Sales Management

75 Training Drills To Build Confidence, Excellence & Teamwork

Michael Delaware

www.ingramcontent.com/pod-product-compliance
Lightning Source LLC
Chambersburg PA
CBHW020154200326
41521CB00006B/365